MEMOIR OF A
FRENCH AND INDIAN WAR SOLDIER

"Jolicoeur" Charles Bonin

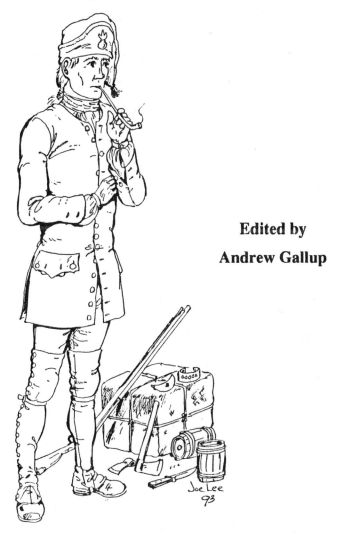

Edited by

Andrew Gallup

HERITAGE BOOKS, INC.

Original Cover Illustration by
Joseph E. Lee

Other Heritage Books from
Andrew Gallup with Donald F. Shaffer:

*La Marine: The French Colonial Soldier in
Canada, 1745-1761*

Published 1993 by

HERITAGE BOOKS, INC.
1540-E Pointer Ridge Place,
Bowie, Maryland 20716
(301) 390-7709

ISBN 1-55613-872-5

A Complete Catalog Listing Hundreds of Titles
on Genealogy, History, and Americana
Available Free on Request

TABLE OF CONTENTS

MAPS

INTRODUCTION

This memoir is unique. It is not only a
first-person account of the French and Indian
War, a scarce commodity, but it is also the
work of a common soldier, rarer still. For
this reason alone, it deserves to be available
to the individual interested in the colonial
history of North America. Beyond this, it is
the work of a Frenchman, a participant on the
other side, as this war is usually viewed by
historians, a viewpoint seldom heard.

Although the author's viewpoint is ethnocentric, he is not a propagandist. He does not
promote a party line. His views are clearly
personal and well considered. Therefore, even
with historical errors, this memoir is important.

The historical errors are many. The fault
may lie with the transcriber(s), translators,
editors, or typesetters. More than likely,
however, the mistakes are in the memory of a
man, advanced in age, trying to flesh-out some
sketchy notes, possibly aided by memoirs of
other participants. Most of the dates are
incorrect, at least if other primary and
secondary sources are accepted. The activity
of one campaign will be included with that of
another or two events will be switched in
sequence. Major fortifications are ignored, as
are certain personalities. The editor of this
edition will try to fill in the gaps and get
the events into line with short introductions
to the appropriate chapters.

The errors lead to the conclusion that
this memoir might be a hoax. Some omissions
are very troubling, such as the total absence
of Detroit during the author's discussion of an
expedition, in which he served, that stayed

there for a considerable length of time. Yet, this is balanced with a number of small inci- dences that fit. As to the mistakes of dates, it is easier to believe that a man's memory after fifty years might be faulty, than a per- son creating a hoax would get so much wrong. Charles Bonin, or J.C.B. as he identified himself, was a marine in Canada, although some of this story might be spruced-up.

The author's motivation must be consid- ered. He all but apologizes for including per- sonal information in what he intended to be a travel guide to Canada. To this end he pro- vides substantial reports concerning geography, natural science, and the native population. His enthusiasm for this area of inquiry seems related, in part, to his arguments concerning the lack of vision on the part of the French government concerning the value of Canada. It should be also noted that the author, while recognizing the United States, seemed to still see the the Great Lakes, western Pennsylvania, and Ohio, as part of Canada, in fact any land west of the Appalachian Mountains.

What do we know about the author? He was once identified as a Monsieur Bonnefons. This was based on the initial of the last name and that Bonnefons was on the staff of Captain Pouchot at Fort Levis, a staff that J.C.B. claims to have been a part, as secretary to this officer. Previous editors have discounted this identification as Bonnefons was an officer. In *La Marine, The French Colonial Soldier in Canada 1745-1761* (Heritage Books, Inc. 1992), this editor and his co-author, identified J.C.B. as "Jolicoeur" Charles Bonin. Our decision to use this was based on a third- hand source. Since then the paper trail led to Donald Kent's, *The French Invasion of Western Pennsylvania* (Harrisburg, 1954) Kent found Jolicoeur Charles Bonin as a *canonnier* listed with the invaders (1755), in the papers of Captain Contrecoeur. As J.C.B. admits to having the nickname Jolicoeur, this is a convincing identification.

What we can believe about J.C.B. is that he was short and probably of slight build. Invitations to parties suggest he knew correct behavior and was probably handsome and/or charismatic. The positions he held and the fortune he was able to accumulate testify to the fact that he was educated, hard-working, and could keep accurate financial records. This indicates he was competent with fundamental arithmetic, and his interest in natural science could suggest a knowledge of advanced mathematics and/or other scholarly pursuits.

J.C.B. was serious about business and does not exhibit a sense of humor. This does not mean he was a stern or hard man. He seems to have quickly become a member of a well-to-do social group, attending parties, balls, and other festivities (including the years before he accumulated his wealth). This would not suggest he was unfriendly. When he "appropriated" supplies for sick soldiers he showed a compassionate trait, although he does not mention any close friends.

This man appears to be competent, highly organized, and self-confident. He is certainly materialistic. His greatest emotional display surrounds the loss of his property. His language is careful when speaking of the Catholic church and missionary activities and he shows an interest in, and objectivity toward, the Protestant faiths he observed in New York City. It seems that if he were to appear today he would adjust to the times and probably make another fortune.

This memoir was first published in Quebec by Abbe H.R. Casgrain in 1887 as, *Voyage au Canada, dans le nord de l'Amerique Septentrionale, depuis l'an 1751 a 1761, par J.C.B.* He worked from a copy of the original manuscript. The Pennsylvania Historical Commission translated and edited Abbe Casgrain's book for *Travels in New France by J.C.B.* published in 1941. It was part of the Frontier Forts and Trails Survey, a Work

Projects Administration (WPA) endeavor. The editors and translators were, Sylvester K. Stevens, Donald H. Kent, and Emma Edith Woods. In 1978, a French edition was published by Editions Aubien Montaigne, *Voyage au Canada fait depuis l'an 1751 a 1761 par J.C.B.*

This edition uses the Pennsylvania Historical Commission's work. The notes of J.C.B. (JCB), and most of the notes of Abbe Casgrain (HRC), and the Commission (PHC) are included and identified by the initials given here. The few not included were explanations of translation difficulties. All notes not followed by one of the three identifications are the responsibility of the editor of this edition, as are the maps. The PHC edition divided the work, a continuous narrative, into chapters. Some changes have been made in these divisions. Chapters have been combined, and in one instance split, to a format which parallels calendar years.

Thanks are due to Donald "Doc" Shaffer, co-author of *La Marine, The French Colonial Soldier in Canada 1745-1761*, for continuing our ongoing debate in the interpretation of the material contained in this memoir, as well as colonial history in general. In much the same way, Terry Todish deserves recognition. As a defender of "the other side" he has added a perspective to this work and other projects. Specifically, Terry was a source of under-standing, and information concerning, the Catholic ways. *Merci* also to Ted Reese for information concerning the route across Saginaw Bay and for being on the same wavelength. To other members of the *Forces of Montcalm and Wolfe* who I may have bombarded with a strange historical fact or question, thanks.

The Pennsylvania Historical Commission and Diane B. Reed, Chief, Division of Publications and Sales, are thanked for allowing their edition to be used.

A.J.G.

PREFACE

Exploration in Canada[1] may be traced back to 1534, when, under Francis I,[2] navigator Jacques Cartier made his first voyage there. He reached only the mouth of the river St. Lawrence, and gave it that name because he entered it on the day they celebrate that saint.

In the following year, he made a second voyage with three ships,[3] and went up the St. Lawrence as far as Montreal, stopping at Quebec. He finally went back to France with only one ship, having lost two ships, by accident,[4] on the voyage from Quebec to Montreal. But Francis I neglected this discovery, because of his heedlessness or his wars. Canada was not settled in his time.

Settlement in Canada began under Henry IV in 1608, when the navigator Samuel Champlain was sent there with several ships and families.[5] He went up the river St. Lawrence and left some families at Tadoussac, which is ninety leagues from the mouth of the river. Finally he went on to Quebec, where he began to build wooden barracks and to have the ground

---

[1]The name Canada comes from the Huron language and means group of cabins (JCB).

[2]Francis I became king in 1515.

[3]*Grande Hermine*, *Petite Hermine*, *Ermillion*.

[4]*Petite Hermine* remained in Canada due to the loss of crewmen from scurvy.

[5]Champlain had been a cartographer for the Sieur de Monts who had established a colony in Acadia in 1604.

leveled for cultivation. There he constructed a fort and settled families.

Three years later, the French government sent over several families, with Jesuits and Recollect missionaries, who were to settle and preach the Gospel to the savages.

In 1665, Louis XIV sent a fleet laden with provisions and merchandise, artillery and firearms. there were on board several families of volunteers and adventurers of both sexes, as well as an entire artillery regiment.[6] Then Quebec grew in population, and villages and towns were formed by grants of land.

The Dutch, Swedes, and Danes also founded settlements in North America south of Canada. The English eventually came and seized the possessions of the Dutch, Swedes, and Danes. It was only under Cromwell's government that the English colonies were peopled and enlarged by emigration of the malcontents in the mother country. These colonies then took the name of New England,[7] as Canada took the name of New France.[8]

New England later became the United States, originally composed of thirteen provinces, which declared themselves independent of the mother country in a general congress held for that purpose on the fourth of July, 1776. This was partly the work of Doctor Franklin.[9] The reason was a Stamp Act passed by the

---

[6]This is probably a reference to the Carignan-Salieres regiment who were infantry.

[7]J.C.B. references to New England include all English North American colonies.

[8]Although Canada and New France are often used interchangeably, New France applies to all the French North American colonies, Canada, Louisiana, Isle Royale, and Acadia.

[9]Benjamin Franklin, born in America, was their ambassador to London and then to France; he returned to America and died in Pennsylvania the 17th of April, 1790 (JCB).

Parliament of England in 1765, which they tried to enforce in the English colonies. On the complaint of the Americans they repealed this act, replacing it by an import duty on tea, which had no greater success. The colonies revolted and declared their independence, causing a war between them and the mother country.[10] This began April 18th, 1775, and ended to the advantage of the colonies, whose independence was recognized by the treaty of September 3rd, 1783.

France helped the Americans to maintain their independence, by the advise of the Council of Louis XVI. The first help given was the three frigates which left Harve laden with cannon and war munitions, in charge of an agent named Beaumarchais.[11] That was before the declaration of war. Some French officers and troops went there a little later. This increased the hatred and animosity of England for France.

I now come to my travels. At the time I came to Canada in 1751, war had not yet been openly declared between France and England, but misunderstanding and jealousy were apparent in Acadia and upper Canada,[12] as will be seen in the course of my travels.

The exactness and truth of this account of my journeys in Canada during my ten years' stay

---

[10] The fighting began on April 19th, 1775, and independence was declared July 4, 1776 or on July 2, if the date of *approval* of the Declaration of Independence is accepted as the act.

[11] Pierre-Augustin Caron de Beaumarchais, the playright who is famous for *The Barber of Seville* and *The Marriage of Figaro* (PHC).

[12] J.C.B.'s geogrgraphy follows the custom of the time and is oriented to the direction of the rivers' current. Consequently, upper Canada is up the St. Lawrence River (to the southwest) and lower Canada is toward the sea.

there, and the comments I have made about its
various scattered tribes, can even today supply
information about the character and extent of
this vast land, about its lakes streams, rivers, its variety of trees, its various kinds of
hunting and fishing; as well as my description
of the habits, customs, and manners of the abo-
riginal inhabitants, known since the first discovery of the country by Jacques Cartier in
1535.[13] This land France lost unwisely by the
treaty of peace in 1763. Since then, it must
have become more profitable in English hands.
It gives them a fur trade, including all varieties.

The historical and descriptive part of
these travels were written on the vary spot,
making use of the moments of repose left me
from my duties. I have gone over it carefully
since my return to France. It may help to make
known the events which gave possession of this
vast land to the English, and may throw some
light on their policy during the invasion. I
have, at least, written nothing which is not
perfectly exact.

In the course of these travels are found
details concerning my personal affairs. I
thought it best to retain them, for they show
how I journeyed through Canada. Perhaps some
readers will not think highly of this book.
Nevertheless, I beg those who may deign to read
it to take into consideration the fact that I
have no other purpose than to explain my position and the circumstances under which I have
written this book, even while I am reporting
the things I have seen.

J. C. B.

---

[13]This refers to the second voyage of
Jacques Cartier, which first made the French
masters of this country. The voyage made by
this navigator in the previous year terminated
at the mouth of the St. Lawrence (JCB).

*J.C.B. may have never heard of Canada at
the time he left his parents' home. If he was
aware of the colony, he did not know of the
state of the competition between England and
France concerning North America. In 1751, an
attempt by the French to attack the
English/Indian trading center at Pickawillany
(Piqua, Ohio) was unsuccessful. Two years
before, Celoron de Blainville led a French
force down the Ohio River to reinforce the
claim of France to the region and to expel
English traders. Each side was engaged in dis-
rupting the trade of the other, with and without the aid of Indian allies. Incidents of
traders being robbed, captured, and killed,
were common.*

YEAR 1751: I left Paris on the 15th of
March to go to La Rochelle, with my father's
permission. I was then eighteen years old.
While I was walking along the road, I came upon
a detachment of one hundred and twenty recruits
led by an officer. He was taking them to the
Isle of Rhee', the place of their departure.
This officer hailed me, and questioned me about
the purpose of my trip, my affairs and financial resources. I replied that I was going,
with my father's permission, to join my uncle

'Three leagues from La Rochelle; four
leagues long and two wide (JCB). The league is
used throughout this memoir. To the mariner
the league equaled 3.45 English miles. On land
it was 2.76 English miles. The reader is
advised to use a modern map to interpret the
distances between towns and forts.

who was captain of the posts[2] at La Rochelle, and had been awaiting me for six months. As for my financial resources, they were not large but sufficient for me until my arrival. Then my uncle would put me in the way of earning more. After this reply, the officer proposed that I travel with him to my destination, where he was going to stay, but on condition that I take care of his things on the way. To this I consented willingly. By my behavior I gained his confidence, and was lodged and fed with him.

When we arrived at La Rochelle, I thanked him and took leave of him in order to go and join my uncle. But when I arrived at his place, I was indeed surprised to learn that the latter had been buried a week before. Because of this misfortune, together with the smallness of my resources for returning to Paris, I decided to find the officer I had just left, and tell him what had happened. The man offered to take me with him to the Isle of Rhee, where he hoped to get me a job from the governor of the citadel. I accepted his offer.

The next day, April 2nd, we crossed in two small sailboats to the Isle of Rhee. As soon as we arrived, I followed the officer, who led his recruits to the citadel and turned them over to the governor. He recommended me so highly that I was at once employed in his office. The pay was small; but in my position I dared not hesitate.

When I had worked about twelve months[3], I was tormented with a desire to travel. I sought information about the best country to

---

[2]The records of La Rochelle list no captain of the posts as dying in that month, as mentioned in the following paragraph (PHC).

[3]The chronology J.C.B. presents would suggest that he worked only two months for the governor. If the twelve month period is correct then he either left Paris in 1750 or he did not arrive in Canada until November 1752.

live in; about Louisiana and Canada, the only
places to which the recruits were then taken
from the Isle of Rhee. The sailors told me
that Canada was more healthy, although its climate is colder. I decided to take their
advise, and to take advantage of the first
sailing, which was not far off. This I did
despite the offers made by the governor, which
I refused, expecting that the voyage would be
more profitable. The orders had come to have a
number of select recruits embark for the colonies of Louisiana and Canada. The first
sailing was to Louisiana, and included two hundred men. Some of these had been companions of
mine on the road. The second sailing was not
delayed, and I took advantage of it.

The 12th of June, I left the Isle of Rhee,
five leagues from La Rochelle, in one of two
small boats which took three hundred recruits
down the Charente River, which is two leagues
from Rochefort. There a vessel[4] was waiting to

---

[4]Originally, barks and rowboats were the
only vessels. Ambition and industry caused men
to construct larger ones to sail in the open
sea. They had at first one mast, then two, and
finally three—on a kind which actually carries
one hundred and twenty cannon or more, carrying
up to thirty-two sails on the several masts.
The bowsprit is on the end of the prow,
fastened on the spur at the bow of the vessel.
The foremast is situated between the bowsprit
and the mainmast, which is in the middle. The
mizzen-mast is the mast of the poopdeck, at the
stern of the vessel. Each mast is lengthen by
two topmasts which also carry a mast, making
three masts one on top of the other, the
highest of which is called the topgallant.
Each of these masts is named by the principal
mast, as, for example—mizzen-topgallant, main-
topgallant, and fore-topgallant, the last of
which is between the bowsprit and the mainmast.
It is the same with topmasts.
A vessel with one hundred and ten cannon

take us to Canada. This vessel was called the *Chariot Royal*. It was a frigate used as a transport, and although pierced for thirty-six cannon, it carried only eight. It was commanded by a naval captain named Salabery.

The 27th of the same month of June; we set sail by a good wind from the northeast, which in two days carried us from the coast of France, setting our course to the west-northwest.

The 31st, the wind became so contrary that we had to use the bowline[5] and tack about for several days. The sea was so rough that we experienced a bad tempest which made us put on a spencer[6]. On this occasion I paid tribute to the sea with a sickness which lasted as long as the weather, nearly five days. All this time I could not eat. At last the wind went down, and the sea became calm. I then recovered my appetite, but, the wind falling completely, the ship stood still, and we were becalmed for two days.

July 15th, a light easterly breeze came up and helped us on our way, but not for long. For, two days later, another storm struck and made us keep on the spencer four more days. In spite of myself, I renewed the tribute to the

---

is two hundred and twenty-five feet high measured from the keel, and draws twenty-five to thirty feet of water. The speed of a vessel under sail is from twenty to thirty feet a second or seven to eight leagues an hour. The longest cable is one hundred and twenty fathoms, the same as one hundred toises [approximately six feet] or six hundred feet (JCB).

[5]The bowline is used to catch the wind at a slant when it comes from the front. The ship is then swung to the right and left. This is called tacking (JCB).

[6]The spencer is two low sails fastened so the wind comes above and below them (JCB).

sea that I had thought paid in full. A rough sea has a disagreeable effect on my stomach.

At last the wind began to shift, the sea became placid, and we could continue our journey, but for only twenty-four hours. A contrary wind then became so strong that we had to tack for three days. After that the wind shifted to the south, and we went on our way to Jacquet Bank, some distance from the Grand Banks of Newfoundland. There, a contrary wind forced us to luff for several days. Then a fierce tempest, also from the west, drove us back about eighty leagues. In these circumstances the rudder line happened to break, and the compass[7] was put out of order. Repairs were quickly made, and four days later we could continue on our way.

August 15th, the wind was again contrary, and we had about three weeks of continual tacking.

The 14th of September, we arrived[8] at the Grand Banks of Newfoundland, in eighty fathoms of water. Immediately the sailors cried, "Long live the King." This is a custom among sailors when they find the bottom.

The Banks of Newfoundland are nine hundred leagues west of France. They are thought to be one hundred and fifty leagues long by about ninety wide, and from fifteen to eighty fathoms deep. They are really a mountain under water.

---

[7]The sea compass or *boussole* is an instrument containing a magnetized needle. Invented by Marco Polo, it was known in France in 1213. It was perfected, in 1302, by the famous Flavio under Philip the Fair. It is said that the first magnet was found on Mount Ida by a shepherd named Magnes. There are two kinds, male and female. The first is blueish and comes from China and Bengal; the second is blackish and is found in Germany (JCB).

[8]Arriving on the Grand Banks is called "banking" in marine terminology. Leaving them is "unbanking" (JCB).

We had much to suffer on these banks from rain and contrary winds, which held us up for several days in spite of all our efforts. This is the most disagreeable and most uncomfortable place in the ocean. The sun seldom appears, and the air is filled with a cold dense fog.

The nearest land is Cape Rouge, which stretches for thirty-five leagues from the east to the west, and is part of the island of Newfoundland, which will be described later.

The wind had just fallen when we arrived on the Grand Banks, and since there was a beautiful calm, the sailors wanted to catch some codfish. But as it was late, they put off the party until the next day, provided the weather was favorable. Unfortunately, there was a heavy rain during the night, along with thunder and lightning. The whole sky seemed to crack open. There was one crash of thunder after another, and the lightning alone through momentarily the light of day into the darkness. The thunderbolts fell near the vessel with a racket like cannon-fire. We were all terrified. During the hour and a half that the storm continued we seemed to be in the trenches. I was ready at any moment to become food for codfish on which we had planned to feast the next day.

After two hours of worry and anxiety, between life and death, the light of day appeared; the thunder and lightning stopped; the wind ceased; and the sea became calm. The sailors repaired the damaged rigging, and we were then able, about noon, to catch some fish. In three days' fishing we took enough cod to feed us for several days.

When it is fresh, the whole of the codfish is good. Nothing of the taste is lost, but it becomes firm when it has been in salt for two or three days. Only the fishermen eat it fresh. The head, tongue, and liver are the best parts. Mixed with oil and vinegar, they make a delicious sauce. Since too much salt is need to preserve these parts, everything that cannot be eaten or preserved during the fishing is thrown into the sea. The largest codfish I have ever seen caught was only three feet long, though others may contend that they are longer.

No other animal, in proportion to its size, has a larger mouth or is more greedy. It is said that all sorts of things, even pieces of broken iron and glass pots, have been found in the stomach of this fish. It is even said that everything is digested; but it is also known that the stomach turns inside out like a pocket, and the fish discharges in this way everything that distresses it. All the codfishermen believe this. Raynal reported it judiciously in his *History of the Two Indies*. The bait for catching these fish is a small fish called capelin which is abundant in these parts.

As the weather continued calm, the crew amused themselves with a baptismal ceremony[9] for the sailors practiced on those who cross the banks for the first time. For this ceremony, they disguise an old sailor with a large fur cap, a pair of high boots, a white wig on his head, a helmet, and a large white false beard. The sailor thus costumed descends from the main-topmast where he is dressed. With the aid of cords and pulleys he slides to the foot of the foremast, where the other sailors receive and conduct him to the foot of the mainmast. Near this they hold the new member to a seat on the edge of a tub filled with water. There Father Terreneuve[10] makes the new member swear to keep the secret from those who have not yet passed this latitude, with a promise never to touch the wife of another sailor. this he must promise at once. If the new member has not taken the precaution of buying drinks, he is immediately tipped into the water

---

[9]Bougainville also mentions this ceremony. He adds that the captain had to ransom his ship from the crew with wine (Bougainville 1964:17 note).

[10]That is what the master of this ceremony is called (JCB).

by the two men holding him. He then emerges to change his clothes. During this time Father Terreneuve goes away, takes off his costume, and reappears, so that the man who was ducked will not recognize him. This is the end of the ceremony, which is quite disagreeable in cold weather, and is only a game played by sailors to get money.

After we had been held up for twelve days on the Grand Banks by contrary winds and calm, a northeast wind came up, and we were able to continue our voyage. It was good sailing all that day; but, during the night, the sailors of the watch cried "luff."[11] We put about. It was high time; for without this precaution the vessel would have been wrecked against the shore, and we and our goods would doubtless have perished. When the vessel had tacked about, we saw at daybreak the danger we had escaped, and as the wind kept up, we had to heave to[12] for four hours.

September 27th, the wind became favorable, and we sailed along, with the island of Newfoundland on our right, passing the Bay of Plaisance, which is the most beautiful harbor on this side of the island. Then we coasted along the islands of St. Pierre and Miquelon which are in the same latitude, and one hundred leagues above Cape Rhee which we have mentioned before.

The 30th of the same month, we doubled Cape Rhee at our right, leaving at the left Cape North, which is the point of Isle Royale. We went to Cape Breton, situated between the 45th and 47th degrees of north latitude, and twenty-five leagues from Newfoundland, which is north of it; forty leagues from the Gulf of St.

---

[11]Luffing is putting the helm about in order to run into the wind. The crew is divided into four watches, each of which watches for four hours (JCB).

[12]To heave to means to stop a ship under sail (JCB).

Lawrence, and fifteen from Acadia and the Isle
St. Jean, which is to the west. After we had
passed between Cape North and Cape Rhee, we
entered the Gulf of St. Lawrence, which is
ninety leagues in length.

The Island of Newfoundland is situated
between the 36th and the 52nd degrees north
latitude. It was discovered in 1534, at the
time of Jacques Cartier's first voyage. The
island is shaped like a triangle and is about
six hundred leagues in circumference. Little
is known about the island; but it contains
steep cliffs, mountains topped with poor wood,
and narrow sandy valleys. The inaccessible
parts of the island are filled with deer, especially in the northern part. Only the Eskimos
go there during the hunting season. The climate is very cold in the north; more temperate
in the south. In 1751, the island contained no
more than five thousand inhabitants, who lived
on codfish which are plentiful in these latitudes.

The coast of Labrador is cut by several
rivers, which come from the north and flow into
the St. Lawrence River at the mouth of the
Gulf. This coast is a station for fishermen.
At the time of my passage, the only inhabitants
were the wild Eskimos, who are said to eat raw
flesh, and flee as soon as they see strangers.
They always live along the seashore because of
fishing.

They fish in little skin boats made of
seal skin sewed in the shape of a change purse,
and closed so tightly that the water is kept
out. These little boats are five feet long,
and hold only one man. When an Eskimo goes to
sea, he sits in the boat with the boat cord
tied around his waist, and, aided by an oar, he
goes out to look for fish. In this way they
pursue seals (sea-dogs or sea-wolves) and,
sometimes, whales, going as far as five or six
leagues out to sea. Several people usually go
together for this sort of fishing. When they
are caught by a squall, they shut themselves in
their canoes and trust to the mercy of the
waves, until a calm permits them to reappear to

continue their hunting or return to shore.
They show more zeal in whale fishing because of
the oil from which they make their drink. They
hunt with great skill. Occasionally, but
rarely, they are the victims. Nevertheless,
though the whale kills them with his tail, and
the sea-dog or sea-wolf with his teeth, the
need for food forces them to brave all these
dangers.

In these latitudes, there are also porpoises of various colors. The gray ones live
in the sea and go up the St. Lawrence River.
The white seek fresh water. The latter are as
large as a cow and yield a cask of oil, almost
as much as the sea-dog and sea-wolf. The skin
of both kinds can be tanned and softened. It
must be scraped thoroughly, because it is very
thick. It is used to make clothes and, more
commonly, to cover trunks. They fish for porpoises in the same way as for sea-wolves or
sea-dogs. At low tide they drive stakes close
together in the mud and sand. They attach a
funnel-shaped net to these with an opening
large enough so that the fish can get in, but
not out. When the tide is low again, it is
left high and dry, and they beat it to death
with a stick.

The sea-dog or sea-wolf (seal) has a head
like a bulldog's. Its feet are very short,
especially the hind feet, which are shaped like
fins. Its forefeet have claws. The animal has
a fur of many colors; some of them weigh as
much as two thousand pounds.

The sea-cow (walrus) is much like the sea
wolf, but larger. It has two lower teeth as
large and as long as an arm. The are slightly
curved for defense. The other teeth are only
four inches long, all beautiful ivory.

After we had sailed fourteen leagues up
the Gulf of St. Lawrence, we passed near Bird
Islands, two small islands, very high, and side
by side. The wind failing us at this place,
three men set out in a shallop to hunt for eggs
on one island where the seagulls, tauyeux,
swans, bustards, and other fowl come to lay
eggs and shed their feathers. Two hours later,

the shallop came back with many kinds of eggs
and beautiful fine eider down.

The 17th of October, after we had tacked
about for several days in the Gulf of St.
Lawrence, an east wind favored us and facili-
tated our passage from the Gulf, leaving to our
right the Island of Anticosti at the mouth of
the river and half its width; and at our left,
to the south, Cape des Rosiers which is above
the point of Gaspe. Here is a steep rugged
cliff thirty fathoms long, four wide and twelve
high. An opening in it forms an arcade through
which a sailing shallop may be sailed. This is
why it has been given the name of Isle
Percee[13], or the Island of Flora.

As we have said, the St. Lawrence River
was named by Jacques Cartier. The river is
said to be forty leagues wide at the mouth, and
one hundred twenty leagues long from its mouth
up to Quebec. From the lower reaches of the
stream, as you go up to Isle aux Coudres,
fifteen leagues from Quebec, you will find
salmon, tuna, shad, trout, emproi, smelt, eels,
mackerel, sole, anchovy, sardines, turbot, all
kinds of rays, cuttlefish, yobage, plaice,
floaters, whose flesh fattens cod, turtles,
sturgeon, black bass, goldfish, cabaillaux,
cariboufish, sharks, porpoises, sea-dogs or
sea-wolves, etc. All these fish go up the
river, except the whale and its enemy the
swordfish. It is a waste of time to catch
sharks, which are not of great value. The
other fish are caught with hooks, harpoons, and
nets *en parquant*.

Fishing for whales and sea-dogs or sea-
wolves is carried on as we have described it.
The whale is killed by harpooning. This fishing results in considerable commerce, as much
for the islands of America as for Europe, which
imports the oil and the ribs, as well as the
furs of the sea-wolf.

---

[13]Error. The Perce Rock is farther on
(HRC).

After we had stayed several days in the lower St. Lawrence because of contrary winds, the northeast wind came. It carried us to Tadoussac, past the Notre Dame Mountains and Mount Louis, and past the Maucelles, three rugged mountains south of the river.

Tadoussac is the first French settlement and a center of the fur trade. It is situated at the mouth of the Saguenay River, which the largest vessels can ascend for twenty-five leagues. There was here, at the time of my passage, a village of Montagnais savages,[14] tributary to the Algonquins and governed by the Jesuit missionaries. We stayed four days, lacking a favorable wind. This settlement, which is no longer a mere savage village, is ninety leagues from the river's mouth, and on the right bank as you go up.

November first, we left Tadoussac, still going up the right bank of the river. We passed Isle Rouge, Isle aux Lievres, and Isle aux Coudres, the last fifteen leagues above Tadoussac. At this last island, we crossed to the left or southern side of the river on account of the dangerous channel, which is about a quarter league beyond Isle aux Coudres. This channel is a narrow rapids formed by an earthquake, which, in 1663, is said to have dislodged a mountain and heaved it upon the

---

[14]The term "savage" is used extensively in this memoir. This is probably a result of a direct translation of the French word *sauvage*. To interpret this in a strictly pejorative sense may be a mistake. This was the common eighteenth-century French term for the Native American people. This is not to say J.C.B. was enlightened. He was ethnocentric and in some cases he uses the term in the manner it would be used today. His frequent use of it with the name of a specific tribe, the Iroquois savages or the savage Ottawa, however, seems more in line with saying, the Iroquois Indians or the Ottawa Indians.

island, leaving in its place a precipice.
After the channel by the Isle aux Coudres, we
came to Cape Tourmente, five leagues above it.
Here we anchored, because of the contrary wind.
We were then only ten leagues from Quebec.

On the third we set sail and went along
the southern side of the river. We skirted the
Island of Orleans to our right, where low tide
forced us to anchor.

The Island of Orleans is seven leagues
long and fourteen in circumference. I have
heard that when Jacques Cartier was here in
1535, he called it the Island of Bacchus,
because there were then many wild grape vines.
In 1676, under the name Orleans, it was made a
barony for Sieur Berthelot who had acquired it
from M. de Laval,[15] first bishop of Quebec. At
that time there were four villages; but at the
time of my visit there were eight, with as many
churches-St. Pierre, St. Laurent, St. Jean, St.
Francois, Ste. Famille, and three others.
There are no longer many vines. Instead, wheat
and grain are grown now on the level and fertile soil. The inhabitants have a comfortable
life there.

Northeast of this island runs an arm of
the St. Lawrence on which only small rowboats
can be used because of the shallow water, especially at low tide. The shore bordering on
this arm is called the Coast of Beaupre. Along
it there are several villages, such as
Beauport, l'Ange-Gardien, la Longue-Point,
Chateau Richer, Ste. Anne, and St. Joachim.

---

[15]Francois de Laval was bishop of Quebec
in 1673. He was then sixty-one years old. He
died May 6th, 1708, at the age of seventy-six
(JCB).

M. de Laval was born April 30, 1623. He
came to Quebec as apostolic vicar in 1659, with
the title of bishop of Petra [Petraea] *in
partibus* [*infidelium*]. Quebec became a
bishopric in 1674 (PHC).

Between Beauport and Ange-Gardien are the Montmorency Falls.

These falls are a cascade which form a beautiful sheet of water about thirty feet wide and forty-eight to fifty feet high. It would seem that such a ceaseless flow must be fed by several lakes or large rivers. It is certain, however, that it is formed by one brook, where in several places the water comes only to the ankles. This brook always flows abundantly, and draws its supply from a little lake called the Lac des Neiges, which is twelve leagues from the cascade. At the same distance is the village of Lorette where the savage Hurons, who are Catholics, have lived since 1670.

On the fourth, taking advantage of the tide, we rounded a point of land to our left, which extended somewhat above Orleans Island and to the north. This is called Point Levis. Then only can the city of Quebec be seen, opposite the cannel by the island, and about a league to the west. We entered the roadstead and anchored at four o'clock in the afternoon, after a difficult voyage of nearly five months. As it was too late to land, we waited until the next day.

On the morning of the fifth we landed. The recruits were taken to the barracks, and I was given lodgings with a wholesale merchant named Samson, who lived in the lower town. I was very well lodged. I remained five days with this honest merchant, who treated me with kindness. In this time I roamed the city and its surroundings, getting from my host any information that I desired.

The city of Quebec, capital of Canada, is built in the form of an amphitheater on a rock forming a point between the St. Charles River on the left and Cape Diamond on the right, on the St. Lawrence River. Point Levis and the Island of Orleans are across the river. There is an upper and lower city. The upper city is fortified on the land side by a strong rampart, which is twenty-five feet high and twenty-five feet thick. This is outside of a good stone wall. Several redoubts and bastions, with the

rampart and wall, make a circuit from the
Plains of Abraham, beside the St. Charles
River, to Cape Diamond.   The rampart, bastions,
and redoubts can hold three hundred and fifty
cannon, all on platforms; but there were then
only one hundred twenty, all iron, and of various calibers.

The beginnings of this city's settlement
go back to 1608 when the navigator Samuel
Champlain[16], then governor, erected wooden barracks, cut trees, and cleared the ground where
it stands today.   Three years later, Jesuits
and Recollects [Recollets] were sent from
France as missionaries to the savages.   This
city, though it had a stone fort built after
the year 1623, when there were not more than
fifty French families, was nevertheless taken
by the English in 1629.[17]   They returned it by
the treaty of St. Germain [-en-Laye] in 1632
[1629?].   Four years after it was returned
(that is in 1636), more families crossed from
France with a fleet carrying supplies.   Then
they began to fortify the city with ramparts,
and it grew in population.

---

[16]He divided it into an upper and lower
city, and died there, greatly regretted, in
1635.   He was succeeded by Sieur de Montmagny.
Next came, in 1672, the Sieur de Frontenac, who
was replaced in 1682 by the Sieur de la Barre.
His successor was the Sieur Denonville.   The
latter was recalled in 1689 and replaced by the
same de Frontenac who was governor in 1672.   De
Frontenac was succeeded by the Comte de la
Galissoniere, next came the Marquis de la
Jonquiere, then the Marquis Duquesne, and the
Marquis de Vaudreuil who was the last governor
(JCB).

J.C.B. omits some of the governors (PHC).

[17]Champlain surrendered to the Kirke
brothers, Jarvis, David, and Thomas, who had
successfully cut off the supplies from France
to Canada.

This city's anchorage is safe and can hold more than a hundred vessels. The anchorage extends for more than a league, measured from the point of Quebec to Cape Diamond, where there is a redoubt armed with cannon trained on the roadstead. The anchorage is from twenty to twenty-five fathoms in depth. The walls of the city are a league in circumference and triangular in form. It cannot be seen from afar because of the mountains which hide two-thirds of it, at a short distance. The city has no entrances on the landward side, except the gates of St. Louis and St. Jean cut through the thick walls.

The lower city has only one street which extends along the river front, high enough on the shore to be in no danger of flooding at high tide. Only merchants and fishermen live there. The street extends only as far as the spot called Sailors leap, which is a very steep place. In the middle of the lower city, there is a small parochial church called Notre Dame des Victories. This was at first a small chapel, built because of a vow made during the siege of 1690.[18] The English were obliged to abandon the siege, because they had not received the help promised by the savage Iroquois, who failed to keep their word.

At the landing place, there is a battery of twelve cannon trained between wind and water on the anchorage. There is a similar battery at Sailor's leap, which is at the far end of the lower city, where the boats winter. A little farther on is the Anse des Mers at the foot of Cape Diamond, where there are wooden shanties in which sailors and fishermen live.

The upper city, which is much larger, is joined to the lower city by a street cut in the rock. On both sides houses have been built. The first structure worth noting at the upper

---

[18]The English force consisted of thirty-four ships and twenty-three hundred men under the command of Sir William Phips.

left is the cathedral and parish church, semi-
nary and bishop's Palace. Next is the Chateau.
All of them overlook the anchorage and face the
Place d'Armes.

The Chateau is built on the rock. Its
entrance is protected by a mere iron railing
enclosing it. There are guardhouses to the
right and left of the inner side of the
entrance, which is a beautiful paved court.
This castle is a fortress flanked by two sali-
ent wings, with a gallery and three batteries
of cannon trained on the anchorage as far as
the Island of Orleans, two leagues away. To
the left, there is an esplanade or redoubt of
natural formation, but artificially beautiful.
It is reached by a gentle slope called Cape
Diamond, of which we have already spoken.

The Place d'Armes, the Government Square,
is a long rectangle surrounded by beautiful
stone houses. Opposite the castle are two convents and churches. One is Recollect; the
other Jesuit. These two buildings are very
beautiful.

Two streets run from the Place d'Armes.
The street called the Rue St. Louis has two
convents, one Recollect and the other Ursuline.
This street leads from the Place d'Armes to
the outside of the city by a gate called St.
Louis, over which one of the two artillery companies[19] lodges. The gate is the entrance to
the city from the suburbs, where there are very
few inhabitants.

The other street, the Rue St. Jean, likewise starts from the Place d'Armes, and like
the Rue St. Louis, terminates with a gate over

---

[19]Offically, there was not a second
artillery company in Canada until 1757. The
artillery company of the Quebec garrison may
have been large enough that it was managed as
two detachments. The Ministry of the Marine
may have delayed a reorganization to avoid the
expense of supporting the new officers a second
company would require.

which there is a second artillery company.
This street is a quarter of the length of the
one almost opposite, which descends to the
lower city.   On the right, going from the Place
d'Armes, is the Rue du Palais.   At the right of
this street is the Hotel-Dieu, a hospital in a
beautiful location overlooking the St. Charles
River.   There are two large wards, one for men
and the other for women.   The beds are clean
and well kept, and the invalids are properly
cared for.   A little lower, to the left of this
street, are the barracks of the troops.   Still
lower, on the same side, is the Rue St. Charles
or de l'Intendance, which turns from the Rue du
Palais and leads to the General Hospital.   The
right side of the Rue de l'Intendance is bor-
dered by houses, at whose rear is the St.
Charles River.   That is why this section is
called St. Charles.

The Indendant's mansion, called the Palace
because the Superior Council meets there, is a
large pavilion.   Its two ends extend and pro-
ject forward several feet.   Midway of the front
there is a double flight of stairs, which is
the entrance. Back of the house there is a
beautiful garden overlooking the St. Charles
River.   This is the most pleasant side, because
the whole street is hidden by a very high hill
called "Abraham," a rugged rock extending half
a league.

Beyond the Intendency, on the same side,
is the house of the King's lieutenant.   Newborn babies, whom libertinism abandons and
humanity welcomes under the name of foundlings,
are usually left at this house.   They are
brought up in the country until they are old
enough to earn their living or they are
adopted, which happens quite often in a place
where the inhabitants are naturally humane and
hospitable.   Beyond this foundlings' home is
the open country.

The General Hospital, built half a league
from the city at the end of an inlet of the St.
Charles River, is the most beautiful building
in the country.   It was built by the efforts
and at the expense of the Bishop of Quebec, St.

Valier[20], who succeeded Sieur de Laval in 1674,
at the time the church of Quebec was made a
bishopric.[21]

This establishment, originally founded to
care for the disabled, has since been used for
invalid soldiers. They are cared for by
thirty-six canonesses, instituted by Bishop de
St. Valier the founder, and all chosen from the
nobility of the country. This hospital is very
healthful and airy, though built in a swamp
near the inlet. In my time, the hospital had
one hundred fifty beds, all endowed by the
wealthiest people of the country. On the other
side of the inlet there are two villages,
Canardiere and Notre Dame des Anges.

In 1753 I visited an aged invalid who was
then one hundred and nine years old. He had
come to Canada from France, in 1665, as a soldier in the regiment of Carignan Saliere. This
had returned from Hungary, where it had been
sent to fight against the Turks. He had shown
great valor in this war. It was intended that
this regiment, as well as several French families, should settle in this country under the
patronage of Minister Colbert,[22] who had
divided among them landed estates, which were
named for the officers. This old soldier could
still express himself very well, but he was
deaf and walked with difficulty. He was called

---

[20]He bought this piece of ground from the
Recollects who once lived there as landlords.
He moved them to their house in the city on the
Rue St. Louis (JCB).

[21]Quebec became a bishopric in 1674, but
M. de St. Valier did not succeed M. de Laval
until 1688 (PHC).

[22]Jean Baptiste Colbert had served as
Intendant under Cardinal Mazarini, the prime
minister of France during the regency of Queen
Anne. Upon the death of Mazarini, Louis XIV
assumed power and Colbert functioned in the
role of prime minister, although without the
title.

Father Carignan, the name of the regiment of which he was the sole survivor. He said he was a Parisian and a penniless old bachelor. He died at the age of one hundred and thirteen, in 1757. Since he came to Canada in 1665, at the age of twenty-one, he lived there ninety-two years. [23]

When I was there, Quebec had not more than fifteen thousand inhabitants, not counting the garrison of twenty-four hundred men. It is the residence of the Governor General who, in 1751, was the Marquis de la Jonquiere [1749-1752]. There was a staff officer, an Intendant who headed the Superior Council, a King's lieutenant, a naval commissary, a treasurer, a provost marshal, a chief surveyor, and a director of forests and waters. [24] Outside the city, between the Gates St. Jean and St. Louis, are the powder magazine and the arsenal, both guarded by a company of musketeers.

There are good merchants in the city, which is very orderly. The people are affable and well-behaved. Drives in an open carriage and gambling furnish amusement in summer. In winter they have carriage races, sled races, and skating races on the ice. They gamble and dance in the evening. Every one had enough to live on without being rich, and liked to make the most of their possessions. The women have the men at their feet, because of their beauty, liveliness, high spirits, and gaiety. They are flirtatious and elegant, and like Europeans better than men of their own country. This is

---

[23]In the original the figures in this paragraph were very much confused, probably because of misprints. They have been altered to make them agree. In the text the dates are, in order from the beginning of the paragraph: 1753, 1665, 1767, and 1644 (PHC).

[24]All who held these positions after Governor de la Jonquiere's time returned to France, where they were finally arrested and prosecuted for embezzlement (JCB).

especially true on the shore of the St. Charles
River, which is called the Coast of Beauport.

After I had looked over Quebec and its
suburbs, I went out on the right-hand side of
the city, looking toward the St. Lawrence. I
went six leagues among the settlements, which I
found unimportant. A league and a half above
the city are the river and village of Cape
Rouge, which have nothing remarkable about
them. The same distance farther up is the St.
Croix River, commonly called the Jacques
Cartier River, because that navigator during
his voyage lost one of his three vessels there
at the mouth of the river, on a huge rock not
visible at low tide. This accident occurred in
1535, more than eighty years before there was a
thought of establishing Quebec. It is evident
that he was shipwrecked at high tide, for otherwise he would have avoided the rock. He
could not have failed to see it at low tide.
Almost opposite this river on the southern
shore of the St. Lawrence, is the village of
Sillery[25] where once French families lived, and
later on the savage Abenaquis and Algonquins
were governed by Jesuit missionaries. Near
this village is a cascade called Chaudiere
Falls.

---

[25]This village dates from 1638, two years
after Quebec's fortifications were begun. Its
name comes from the former commander of Malta.
He built without much success because the
French families domiciled there preferred to
live on the northern side of the river (JCB).

Due to his poverty, J.C.B. joins the col-
ony troops and he provides some details of this
organization. Apparently, qualifications for
the artillery company were stricter than those
of the infantry. There was much free time for,
learning to dance, social events, drinking with
fellow soldiers, and outside employment. The
author seems to have been quickly accepted into
Canadian society.

At the end of this chapter J.C.B. provides
information concerning the rivalry with England
in North America. He mentions the troubles in
Acadia (Nova Scotia) and hints at the conflict
over the Ohio country. In 1752, Ottawa
Indians, led by Charles Langlade, and accompa-
nied by a few marines, successfully attack the
trading center at Pickawillany. Although
J.C.B. notes the arrival of the Marquis
Duquesne, he does not speak of the activity of
the new governor in preparing the colony for
war. He soon would be a part of it.

In five days, I had visited the most
interesting places. I was then forced to give
up my life of needy idleness. I therefore
determined to take up the military profession,
which, though seemingly severe, would nevertheless relieve me at once of my difficulties.

This decision was compelled by circumstances. I felt an inclination for a more
lucrative occupation. But I made up my mind
and of my own free will left the merchant with
whom I had been boarding, going at once to the
artillery commander' to enlist in that company,
because, after making inquiries, that branch of

'This may be Mercier who is mentioned
often in this memoir.

the service seemed more to my liking. They
were paid sixteen to eighteen francs[2] a month.

When I informed this officer of my wish to
enlist, he said I was unfit and not tall enough
to enter the artillery service.[3] Fortunately
for me, three women[4] were there, who were willing to take an interest in my welfare, because
of my well-bred air. After he had asked me
various questions, which I answered frankly to
the best of my ability, the officer decided to
enlist me as a gunner, at the request of these
ladies. They thanked him, and to show their
satisfaction, proceeded to give me the nickname
of "Jolicoeur."[5] A louis of provincial paper
money[6] accompanied it, which one gave to me. I
accepted it very willingly, for I was penniless. At the same time I received the commander's orders to be present at the review by the
Governor General, which was to be held the next
day, November the 12th, on the Place d'Armes.
The recruits were to be incorporated into the
various companies of troops garrisoned in the

---

[2]J.C.B. seems to use francs and livres
interchangeably. The livre was the unit of
currency used in this period.

[3]At this time the commander was probably
concerned with the service of the heavy
fortification guns. A 24-pounder weighed three
tons. This would require a gun crew of men
with some strength.

[4]One was a captain's wife, and the other
two, captain's widows (JCB).

[5]Nicknames (nom de guerre) are, of course,
common to military service. This custom was
observed in the marines. The PHC translated
Jolicoeur as Sweetheart.

[6]Coins were continually in short supply in
Canada. On a number of occasions the colonial
government issued "card money" in a variety of
denominations, in at least one instance written
on the back of playing cards. Each bill was
hand written and signed by the colonial
officers.

city and not yet formed in regiments, because
they were reckoned free companies of the
marine. I was present at the review. All the
troops were under arms in three lines, which
included eighteen companies. The recruits were
unarmed and formed two lines.

The Governor, accompanied by the staff
officer, arrived about noon. When they had
assigned me my place at the end of the artillery companies, which performed the duties of
grenadiers, the inspection began. When the
commander spoke of me to the governor, he
looked me over. That was all as far as I was
concerned. He went on to the other companies
and finally to the recruits. There, each captain, according to his age, beginning with the
gunners, took the number of men assigned to
him. The commander of the gunners chose ten
men without counting me, and the other captains
did the same. When the selection of men was
finished, each company retired with its
recruits. I was one of five taken into the
second company, which was lodged over the Gate
St. Jean. the next day we were given our
clothing and equipment.

As usual during the review, a great many
persons, even the most distinguished people of
the city, were attracted by curiosity. I saw
there with pleasure my three patronesses, who
made much of me and gave me eighteen francs in
silver. There generosity was a happy omen for
me. When I joined the company, I gave the
eighteen francs I had just received to pay my
initiation fee, as was the usual custom. It
secured me friends in the usual soldier way,
but I valued them only as far as they could
serve my interest, and without making a habit
of frequenting taverns with them.

They gave me as a bedfellow (for they
slept double) a Parisian with a handsome and
pleasing face, who had the vices of gambling
and drink. He was also quarrelsome and ill-
natured, often drawing his sword without the
slightest provocation. In time, however I
began to acquire so much influence over him,
that I subdued his fits of passion by my very

presence. In the morning he was good-natured
and amiable, especially toward women, whom he
studied to deceive. He was extremely fond of
dancing, at which he was an expert. He gave me
a liking for it, by taking me with him to balls
and teaching me its principles. At the end of
three months I became, under his supervision,
almost as proficient in that art, which helped
at least for a time to turn him from his vices.
Later, when I neglected him somewhat, he took
up his old habits. He took advantage of my
kindness to him by wearing my clothes and helping himself to my money, to the point where I
was unable to go out. This conduct cooled my
friendship, and I decided to break with him.

During the month of December, a merchant
offered me a place in his store to keep books
and learn his business.[7] I took it without
hesitation because I had vowed, viewing the
uncertainty of the future, that I would learn
everything possible that I might need to use.
I knew that a man who has but one aim might
find himself embarrassed if that should fail
him. I then began to work with the merchant,
who, finding me full of zeal for his interests,
became my friend. I pleased him so much that
he worked for my discharge from the army. This
benevolent act encouraged me to show him my
great gratitude, which I did with all my heart.
He took all the steps he thought necessary for
my discharge, but they were fruitless. I was
told, indirectly, that this good man intended
to take me into his business as soon as he had
procured my discharge, and to give me the
store, and his only daughter in marriage. She
was a beautiful, well-educated young girl. On

---

[7]Marines had duty, usually as guards,
every fourth day. Although they were on call
and had to perform ceremonial and other
functions, they had much free time. This gave
them the opportunity to work for wages in
private business or on government and military
projects, such as roads and fortifications.

this occasion fortune was unkind, and I regretted then that I had enlisted.

I had not lost sight of my three
patronesses, whom I visited several times during the course of the winter months. They had
always received me with kindness that was real
and sincere. One day I unexpectedly met three
officers, their relatives,[8] who had seen me
there several times. They reproached the
ladies about me, although they were perfectly
free to receive me at their homes. When these
three relatives could not persuade the ladies
not to receive me any more, they took another
way which succeeded. They went to the artillery commander, and asked him to use his
authority to have me discontinue my visits to
these ladies. An order reached me instructing
me to appear before the commander. When I
arrived there, I received a warning with a
threat of imprisonment. Since I could not dis-
obey my commander's order without punishment, I
had to submit. I wrote immediately to the
ladies that I was most unhappy to discontinue
my visits; but that, against my will, I had to
obey an official order. I received no answer,
but some days later I learned that these ladies
had quarreled with their relatives, and I was
still the more sorry to have been the involun-
tary cause.

Year 1752: The month of March of this
year, Governor General de la Joncquiere, who
had succeeded Comte de la Galissoniere, died in
Quebec.

A short time later, the birthday of the
Duke of Burgandy, the Dauphin's son, was cele-

---

[8]By the 1750's, the officers of the marine
troops were almost all Canadian-born. These
men were often sons of current or former marine
officers. Records show that the families were
related by marriage and marine officers are
often shown as godfathers of children of other
officers.

brated.[9]   Preparations were made for a display
of fireworks, the artillery taking charge by
order of their commander.   Consequently, I was
one of the workmen chosen, which obliged me to
leave the merchant for whom I worked.   He had
treated me like an adopted child.   It took us
three months to get the display ready.   The
13th of July was the day set aside for the
fireworks.   Twelve gunners were chosen for setting them off.   I was one of them.

When the day arrived, we were dressed in
clothing and hoods of skin as a precaution,
which was necessary.   For, while we were
waiting for the signal to start the fireworks,
a lighted wick carelessly handled set fire to a
rocket.   Its explosion set off a box in which
there were a hundred pieces.   Going off, they
set fire to many others, and soon all the fireworks in the display were in flames, and burned
part of the structure.

The fire was over in a quarter of an hour.
Five gunners were burned to death, and four
seriously injured.   Since I was in charge of
the properties, I was less exposed, yet not far
enough away to escape the explosion.   The rock-
ets flew in every direction, and hemmed me in,
so that I was forced to remain motionless in my
place.   I was nevertheless wounded, but only
slightly in the shoulder, and my clothing was
partially burned.   When the violence of the
fire had subsided, I could leave my refuge to
go to the half-burned platform, I was not a
little surprised to find so many killed, and
myself one of three survivors.   Many of the
spectators were likewise surprised that all of

---

[9]The Dauphin, father of the Duke of
Burgandy, was the son of Louis XV and father of
Louis XVI.   The Duke of Burgandy was the elder
brother of Louis XVI.   He was born in
September, 1751, was baptized under the name of
Louis Joseph Xavier of France, and died at
Vesailles, the 22nd of March, 1761, nine and a
half years old (JCB).

us had not perished. Every one congratulated us, and the intendant sent us each a donation of fifty francs.

Since these fireworks were not successful, it was decided to plan another display on the St. Charles River, opposite the Intendent's house, the first of September following. This display was prepared more quickly than the first one, because all the material was on hand, as well as some fireworks left over from the first display. I was again employed at this work.

The day arrived for the fireworks, I had another little accident which was not less perilous, but just the opposite of my first mishap. My work was to go in a boat to start a display piece representing the Dauphin, which was set up on one of the long sides of the exhibition platform. When the time arrived, I hurried too much when I jumped into the boat that was to take me over, and I fell in the water. Luckily, the boatman pulled me out promptly; I escaped with a wetting, and, without being discouraged, I carried out my task. I was afterwards taken back to shore, where I had to change clothes. My accident was reported to the Intendant, and he sent me two louis more than the twenty-four francs given to each of the twenty gunners employed in this celebration.

During this season, the turtle doves are very abundant in Quebec and its surroundings, especially during the month of September when these birds usually fly over for a fortnight, seeking a warmer climate. They are so numerous that they seem to be a heavy cloud, and they often fly so low that it is easy to kill them with guns or even clubs. We killed so many that they sold for twelve cents a dozen. Still some wanted them plucked, as a result of which we gave away a dozen unplucked with another dozen plucked. In season these birds are usually very plump, and taste very sweet, even though they are birds of passage. They make a very good soup and can be cooked like pigeons.

It was not long before the Marquis Duquesne, vice admiral of the fleet, arrived from France to replace Governor de la Joncquiere, deceased. His first act was to acquaint himself with the state of provincial affairs. He learned his predecessor had had disputes with the English governor (Cornwallis)[10] commanding at Halifax,[11] a city in the territory of Acadia, which the English called Nova Scotia.

Cornwallis had in 1749 succeeded Mascarene,[12] who used to command here. In 1760 (sic)[13] Cornwallis began war on the French living along the French Bay in Acadia. The same year he drove the Acadians out, and, along with the savage Abenaquis who used to live here, they fled to the neighborhood of Quebec. Cornwallis then built a mined fort at the end of the bay, in a place called Chibouctou in the Abenaquis language, and Beaubassin in French.[14] This act forced Governor de la Joncquiere to make reprisals by building two forts, one opposite Beaubassin, called Beausejour; and the other, called Gaspareaux, at the entrance of Green Bay. All remained peaceful after the

----

[10]Edward Cornwallis, uncle of Lord Cornwallis (PHC).

[11]Halifax was built on Chebucto (or Chibouctou) harbor (PHC).

[12]Paul Mascarene, a military engineer, became acting governor in 1739.

[13]This probably refers to the British expedition to Beaubassin (1750) to fortify the Isthmus of Chignecto. This was opposed by the Abbe le Loutre who burned the Acadians homes in the face of the British and collected enough men to force the British back to their boats.

[14]Fort Lawrence was built in 1750, at the head of Chignecto Bay. The inhabitants of Beaubassin were not driven out by the English, but were induced to leave by the missionary, Le Loutre. The English were occupying territory which had been ceded to them (PHC).

agreements seemed to be reached between France and England. (Agreements that were not sincere on the part of the English, as will be seen later.)

Conditions were different in upper Canada toward the Ohio where Governor de la Joncquiere, as a result of what his predecessor Sieur de la Galissoniere had begun, was forced to send detachments of regulars and Canadian troops to drive out the groups of English traders who had settled there in 1750. In 1751 this governor caused the arrest of four traders who were brought to Quebec, where they were questioned in June, and then sent to France.[15] They were for some time detained in La Rochelle. Here they claimed protection from the English ambassador, Lord Albemarle, who obtained their liberty as a personal favor from the Minister of Marine.

During the remainder of the year 1752, I went on with my work for the same merchant, whom I had left only to prepare the fireworks. My evenings were spent enjoying society balls, where I was well received.

---

[15]This may be a reference to the traders taken in an attack on the village of Pickawillany (Piqua, Ohio) in 1752, by Charles Langlade and a force of Ottawa and Ojibwa Indians.

III

J.C.B. goes west for the first time. He is a member if the expedition that begins what might be seen as the first campaign of the final French and Indian War. The invasion of the Ohio country by English traders, which the French and Indians believed would be followed by settlers, drove them to build forts to protect their economic interests and the communication link with Louisiana. The first of the new forts, Fort Presque Isle (Erie, Pennsylvania) provided some protection to the direct water route to Detroit, but its primary purpose was to guard the supply route to the forks of the Ohio. In the following year Fort Duquesne would be built at that location closing the Ohio region to the English. Forts Le Boeuf and Machault[1] were established at strategic points between Fort Presque Isle and Fort Duquesne.

Year 1753: In January, Governor Duquesne, wishing to follow his predecessor's plans decided to send a detachment of four hundred volunteers, half regulars and half Canadians, to the upper country to drive out the English traders, and to overawe the savage tribes. This detachment, armed and equipped, left Quebec the 30th of the same month by land. It was commanded by Captains St. Pierre, Pean, and

---

[1] The French established themselves at the junction of French Creek and the Allegheny River in late 1753 using the cabins of John Frazier. Fort Machault was not completed until 1754.

Le Mercier.[2] As this detachment had eighteen
gunners, I was included.

The first day, we reached Cape Rouge River
where there is a village. Then we went to
Jacques Cartier River of which we have already
spoken; from there to Point aux Trembles, which
is seven leagues from Quebec, and is a pleasant
enough village. Here we spent the night. The
next day we continued on our way, passing the
villages of Batiscan and Port Neuf, ten leagues
from Quebec. Then we reached Deschambault
which is seven leagues above, and from there
the town of Three Rivers, thirty leagues distance from Quebec. The parishes of these villages are pleasantly situated on the right bank
of the St. Lawrence going up.

The town of Three Rivers is located on the
same side. It was founded in 1645[3] (nine years

---

[2][Jacques] Legardeur de St. Pierre did not
become commander of the expedition until
December, 1753, after the death of Marin, the
original commander. But St. Pierre was a
relative of Legarduer de Repentigny, who was
with Marin. J.C.B. may have confused the two
(PHC). St. Pierre died at the battle near Lake
George (1755) where Baron Dieskau was defeated
by Sir William Johnson.

The commander, Pierre Paul Marin, was an
experienced frontier officer and, apparently,
drove the men of this expedition hard as
evidenced by the sickness they suffered.

Michel Jean Hugues Pean became Town Major
of Quebec in 1756 and was included in the
arrests of corrupt officials upon returning to
France. His wife was reputed to be the
mistress of Bigot, the Intendant.

Francois Le Mercier was a military
engineer and the commander of colonial
artillery in Canada. He was also involved with
the Bigot group. He was the engineer who
designed Forts Presque Isle, Le Boeuf, and
Duquesne the following year.

[3]Three Rivers was founded in 1634 (PHC).

after the fortification of Quebec was begun) on a flat and sandy bank of the three rivers which give it a name. These rivers, coming from the north, empty into the St. Lawrence. Iron mines are located there. Forges have been set up at their entrances, in which iron bars, pots, kettles, and other utensils are manufactured. The city owes its existence to the facility with which the northern savages could bring their furs to exchange for French merchandise. But this location, which in its origin seemed advantageous, never had a population of more than fifteen hundred, because the fur trade soon shifted away to a more distant point. The town had then its own governor, named Rigaud[4], a staff officer,[5] and six companies in garrison. It was not fortified, and it had a parochial church, a Recollect convent, and a convent of Ursuline nuns dependent on the Quebec convent, who served in a hospital. The surroundings of this town are fertile and well cultivated. The woods are a short distance from the city.

When we had stayed for two days in this town, we continued our journey by land, still following the bank of the river. A little farther up the river from Three Rivers is Lake St. Pierre, a widening of the St. Lawrence River.

---

[4]Sieur Rigaud de Vaudreuil, 1703-1779, was the brother of the last governor general of Canada, Pierre de Rigaud, Marquis de Vaudreuil-Cavanal. He served under General Montcalm during the war as the commander of colonial troops.

[5]The staff officer probably refers to the town major. In Canada, only Quebec, Montreal, Three Rivers, and Detroit, had this position. This was due to the organization of the marines on a company basis which allowed for no rank higher than captain. At these site, however, there were more than one company in garrison making an overall commander and command structure necessary.

It is three leagues long and its greatest depth is twelve feet. It abounds with fish. Three leagues from Three Rivers is the village of La Valtrie, then Saint Sulpice, next Repentigny, and at last Montreal. We arrived there on the 14th of February.

All the villages just mentioned seem pleasant, but not wealthy. It is the same with those north [should be south] of the river, which are, from Quebec on: Becancourt, Varennes, Boucherville, Le Tremblai, Sorel, and Longueuil.[6]

The town of Montreal is on an island ten leagues long and four wide, formed by the St. Lawrence which surrounds it. In the Huron language it was originally called "Hochelaga," meaning two mountains. It still had that name when Jacques Cartier was there in 1535 with only two ship's boats, leaving his two remaining vessels in Lake St. Pierre near Three Rivers. The navigator found only straggling villages of savage Hurons, who welcomed him. It was only then that he named it Mount Royal, from which has since been derived the name Montreal, because of a mountain with two peaks, only a league away.

In 1650, several families began to settle on this island in wooden cabins.[7] They called their settlement Ville Marie, under the auspices of the priests of the St. Sulpice Seminary in Paris, who became owners of the whole island. It was deeded to them by the savage Hurons, the latter then going to the mainland north of the city. The seminarists gave up their property rights to Louis XIV, who left them only the lordship of the island.

---

[6]Most of these villages are named for officers of the Carignan Regiment, which has been mentioned (JCB).

[7]The first settlers arrived at Montreal in 1642. The formal grant of the island was in 1640 (PHC).

In 1652,[8] Montreal was built and laid out
formally, under the care of Sieur de
Maisonneuve[9] who was its first commander. It
is in the shape of a long rectangle. At first
it was surrounded by strong palisades, but some
years later this was replaced by a good
crenellated stone wall, fifteen feet high.

The population of this pleasant city in my
time did not exceed eight thousand inhabitants.
It had its own governor, a staff officer, garrison troops, a beautiful Place d' Armes,
stores dealing in commodities and food, a
cathedral, a parish church, a seminary, two
convents for men, one Jesuit and the other
Recollect, another for nuns of the congrega-
tion, a general hospital, and an Hotel-Dieu.
This city was the third and the last which was
in existence during my stay in Canada. There
was no other French settlement beyond it,
except the posts where the garrisons were maintained.

Though only sixty leagues from Quebec,
Montreal is four degrees warmer in temperature.
The climate is very cold and healthful in winter; the sky is always clear. In January and
February the Reaumur thermometer ordinarily
drops 27 to 33 degrees. In summer, the heat
reaches the other extreme.

The people of Montreal are much more
lively, brave, ardent, enterprising, and more
warlike than the people of Quebec. They claim
to be invincible, which has not however kept
them from occasionally being surprised by the
savage Iroquois. But since they are good
fighters and used to savage ways, it is more
difficult to vanquish them. They are good
voyageurs, guiding their canoes skillfully,
singing all the time. They spend freely what
they earn on their trips with traders, who go
every year to barter with the savage northern

---

[8]1642 (PHC).
[9]Paul de Chomeday, Sieur de Maisonneuve.

tribes.   These trading trips sometimes take
more than a year.

The people of Montreal call the people of
Quebec "Sheep."   The latter are really gentler
and less vainglorius.   They retaliate by calling the people of Montreal "Wolves," a term
which fits them well enough, as their time is
spent mostly in the woods with savages.   The
people of Quebec, on the contrary, are mainly
fishermen, and deal only with the Europeans,
which makes them more civilized; but they are
just as courageous as the others.   The
Canadians are in general sincere, kind-hearted,
and hospitable.   Crime, murder, or robbery does
not exist among them, but the majority are
uneducated.

Between the Island of Montreal and the
mainland to the north, is another island called
the Isle Jesus, where the River des Prairies
flows, in which there is a rapid and a waterfall called the Recollect Falls.   This is in
memory of a monk of that order who was drowned
there, in 1655, on his return from a mission to
the northern Hurons.   The Isle Jesus begins
near the village of Chenaye, which is a little
above Repentigny, and ends at the upper part of
the Lake of Two Mountains.   Here the Thousand
Islands are located, and here the Outaouais or
Grand River (called the Ottawa by the English)
enters.   More will be told of this later.   The
River des Prairies is only a channel separating
the Island of Montreal from Isle Jesus.

The second of March, after we had stayed
several days in Montreal, when I got the information about which I have just told, we were
reinforced with two hundred militiamen.   the
next day, the third, we embarked in bateaux and
canoes,[10] and crossed from Montreal to Isle

---

[10]Canoes are the most frequently used
water transport in upper Canada, because they
are light enough to make the necessary portages
around the frequent rapids.   They are made of
light wooden strips as thick as a strong lath,

Perrot, which is two leagues above. We skirted
this island, leaving it to our right on the
north. It separates the Lake of the Two
Mountains, which is still farther north, from
Lake St. Louis, a little to the south above
Isle Perrot.

We arrived at the rapids of the Cascades.
To avoid them, we had to make a portage to the
right into a place called the "Trou." This
portage is very bad, and we had to carry our
canoes and baggage on our backs. As we could
not carry the bateaux, we emptied and pulled
them through the water by a rope, with men
pushing at the back. In this way we avoided
another portage nearby, called the "Bruisson,"
which is a sheet of water flowing over a shin-
gled beach having a three-foot fall. We camped
above the "Trou." Opposite and to the south is
St. Louis, a village where the savage Iroquois
live who are governed by the Jesuits.

These Indians were formerly two leagues
farther down at a place called Prairie de la
Madeleine. The Jesuit missionaries brought
them to Sault St. Louis to get them nearer the
other villages of the same tribes, called

---

bent half double, then curved in a half circle.
they are placed four or five inches apart, with
the ends attached to a slender pole bound with
wooden straps like barrel hoops. five
crossbars are placed along the inside of the
canoe, which is from twelve to twenty feet in
length, or more. These crossbars hold the
canoe open. It is from seven to eight feet
across at the widest part, and narrows toward
both ends. The framework is covered on the
outside with birch bark, sewed together with
wooden withes. The seams are then covered with
gum or resin to keep them watertight. These
boats are very light. Loaded, they are easily
managed by two men, one at each end. More men
can be put in if they are seated. If they are
large, four men can carry the empty canoes; if
small, two men are enough (JCB).

Mohawks, Cayugas, and Onondagas, all untamed
and unrestrained. The missionaries hoped to
convert them to the faith. There zeal brought
them only a small number of converts, whom they
baptized and instructed in the Catholic religion; but at the cost of lives of both missionaries and converts. Those savages who were
still idolators made war against the savages
who left their villages to go to the St. Louis
Mission, considering them deserters. They also
made war on the missionaries, three of whom
were taken prisoner and burned at the stake,
together with some of their converts. Their
faith was firm under the torments inflicted on
them by savages who were both enemies and their
relatives. Because of this, the missionaries
preached that, since their death, miracles had
been performed at the tombs of these martyrs
for those who had faith. The lame and the
paralyzed have been cured by the trip to Sault
St. Louis to pray at the new saints' tombs,
where their bodies certainly could not be
interred, since they had been burned.

In the neighborhood of Montreal, however,
four fetes are celebrated in honor of the four
savage martyrs of the village St. Louis, and
some of the neighboring parishes go in proces-
sion once a year, to sing high mass.

The saints venerated are:

Catherine Tega Kouiata, born 1656, daughter of a Mohawk father and an Algonquin mother.
She was baptized and given the name Catherine
on Easter day, 1676. She made the vow of chastity and died on Holy Wednesday, in 1678, at
the age of twenty-two.

Etienne Teganauokoa, Cayuga Indian, married, and father of six children, came to the
Falls when he was thirty-five years old. While
hunting during the year he came there, he was
taken prisoner by the men of his tribe. He was
taken to their village and burned at the stake,
in August, 1690, the year of his capture.

Francoise Gouana Tenha, an Onondaga woman,
taken prisoner while she was fishing, was
burned by her family, The date is not given.

Marguerite Garangoa, a young woman, twenty-four years old and the mother of four children, from the village of Onontaque, baptized when she was thirteen years old, captured by the Indians of her village, and burned at the stake in 1693.

The day after we camped above the "Trou," we went to the Cedars-small islands, by which the channel is very treacherous. Two leagues above is Coteau du Lac where we made a portage. Half a league farther is Lake St. Francois, which we followed down its length, which is nine leagues, while it is three leagues in width. It teems with huards," a kind of cormorant whose mournful cry is very unpleasant. The voyageurs claim its cry is the forecast of rain. The next morning it really did rain, so hard that we could not continue our voyage. We had to camp for two days, but did not, however, waste our time, for we hunted deer and ducks. We killed more than we needed for food, as a part of it spoiled.

When the rain stopped, we continued our journey. We passed the Chenaux-small islands where there is a rapids. After this, there is another called Mouinet rapids, very bad, and necessitating another portage. Finally the Long Sault rapids, half a league in length, are reached, where we again had to make a portage by dragging and pushing the bateaux with ropes and poles. These rapids, which extend for nearly two leagues, can be run in canoes and bateaux only on the southern side through the rocks. The distance is covered in less than fifteen minutes through very swift and turbulent water, in the midst of rocks that must be avoided to escape destruction. It is usually the guides from Montreal who run these rapids, since they are the most accustomed to its passage. They use it for trading trips.

"Black-throated diver (Colymbus articus) (PHC).

Seven leagues above the Long Sault, is the Rapide Plat, and five leagues beyond, are the Galots, the last rapids we found. Past the Galots are a succession of three small islands of the same name, one after the other. Of these, the farthest to the south is Isle Levis of which we shall speak later. Two leagues higher up is La Galette, where the fort of the same name was built by the French. This is now only a storehouse guarded by but fifteen men, and the post is reckoned to be fifty leagues from Montreal. We camped opposite on the north. Finally we passed the Thousand Islands, so named because of their great number. They are so close together that the channels between them are all deathtraps. In the former times these aided the Iroquois in their wars with other savage tribes, and with the French.

At one time the Iroquois[12] were a very populous nation who lived in the north of Canada. In the end they were obliged to move to the south. The divided into five tribes, all Iroquois, and called Senecas, Cayugas, Onondagas, Oniedas, and Mohawks. These villages differ only in language. They are all of a turbulent disposition; revengeful, and loving war, which they have always carried on successfully, and with more caution than the other savage tribes. This is one of the main reasons for their superiority to their enemies, who are, however, just as brave, and who have might have crushed the Iroquois by their overwhelming numbers. One of the reasons for the superiority of the Iroquois is that when they went to war, they would take the precaution of placing sentinels around their encampment. They

---

[12]It was the Iroquois who persecuted the missionaries most, though there were some Christians among them. Of them it has been said, they came like foxes, attacked like hares, and fled like birds. It can be added that they have since then degenerated a great deal, though they are still warlike (JCB).

remained there very quietly. This the enemy tribes do not do, especially the Erie tribe who always let themselves be surprised, causing their defeat. The Hurons and Ottawas, as brave warriors as the Iroquois, after fighting with the latter many times, retired to the north for peace. But this did not keep the Iroquois from warring continually on the French, to who they appeared friendly as long as it was to their advantage.

After we had passed the Thousand Islands, we passed three others, Isle aux Cochons, Isle aux Cedres, and Isle aux Cerfs. Then we entered a bay which is northeast, at the outlet of Lake Ontario. In the bay is Fort Frontenac, called Catarakoui by the savages and Canadians, and later called Kingston by the English.[13] We camped for three days under the cannon of this fort, which was named for Governor de Frontenac. He had it built in 1672,[14] as much to favor his treaty with the northern tribes as to hold in check the Iroquois with whom they were at open war. Their might, and nearness to the rear and to the surroundings of the settled territory, helped them to make war on the northern tribes as well as on the French voya-geurs. The establishment of this fort gave more help to the French in continuing their war on the Iroquois, which finally forced them to move south to the borders of New York.

Fort Frontenac was destroyed in the course of the war, and was rebuilt some time later, by order of the same governor, on the former site. The ground is marshy, and it had to be cleared and made level. In 1753 this post, which had been the key to the upper country, was no longer used as a warehouse; though it still had eight cannons and thirty men in garrison. The marsh behind it was only cleared to a quarter

---

[13]American Loyalists founded Kingston in 1782 (PHC).
[14]1673.

of a league. Fish and game are plentiful in this territory.

March 25th, we left this post, and crossed to the south side of the mouth of Lake Ontario. This lake is said to be one hundred and sixty leagues long and three hundred leagues in circumference. It is oval in form. Two small two-masters were at that time used to carry merchandise and war munitions. They came back and forth from the further end of the lake to its outlet. The first ships on the lake were built under the direction of Sieur de la Salle, governor of Montreal.[15]

After we had crossed to the lower side of Lake Ontario, a distance of two leagues from north to south, we passed the river de l'Assumption, the River des Sables, the River de la Planche, and the River de la Grande Famine. The last so named because a detachment of Canadians under the command of Sieur de la Barre[16] was surprised there by a party of Iroquois, whose only hostile action was to take away their food and supplies, which reduced them to famine, and forced them to return by land. We camped near that river, taking the usual precautions, because of its nearness to some Iroquois villages and to the English Fort

---

[15]De La Salle was never governor of Montreal. He was commander at Fort Frontenac (HRC).

La Salle was, however, a large landholder in the vicinity of Montreal, receiving a grant from the Sulpicians on the north shore of Lake St. Louis.

[16]Joseph-Antoine le Febvre de La Barre replaced Frontenac as governor in 1682. In 1684, he led a force west to quell the troubles caused by the Iroquois. By the time he reached Fort Frontenac his command was sick and when he met the Iroquois in council he was forced to obey their demanded he return to Montreal. When word of this reached Paris he was recalled.

Oswego,[17] called Chouaquin by the French,
located on the lake bank at the mouth of a
river of the same name.

The next day we continued our journey, and
passed the fort three leagues out to escape its
cannon, which might have fired on us. Since
the wind was favorable we went under sail, and
camped ten leagues above Bay des Goyogouins.
the next day we reached River des Tsonotouins,
which is fifteen leagues beyond. Then we came
to River aux Boeufs, and from there to the
Niagara which we reached on the 11th of April.

---

[17]Fort Oswego was established on the shore
of Lake Ontario at the mouth of the Oswego
River. Its purpose was to interrupt the French
fur trade with the western Indians, and
redirecting the furs in favor of the Albany
traders. As strategic military location, it
stood on the line of communication and supply
between central Canada and the western posts.

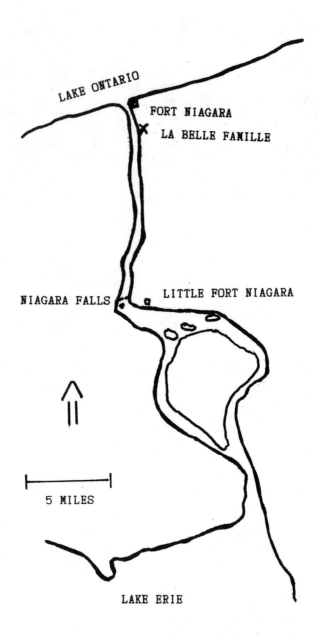

LAKE ONTARIO

FORT NIAGARA

LA BELLE FAMILLE

NIAGARA FALLS

LITTLE FORT NIAGARA

5 MILES

LAKE ERIE

IV

*J.C.B., probably due to his intelligence
and his small size, was fortunate to become a
storekeeper at Fort Presque Isle. This may
have saved his life, as the men working on the
fortifications died in great numbers. Captain
Pierre Paul Marin drove the workers hard and
fed them on salt meat and hard bread. The
author mentions, but does not dwell on this,
preferring to highlight his own charitable
actions and the pleasures of turkey hunting.*

Fort Niagara, situated at the southern or
upper end of Lake Ontario, was originally
called Denonville. It is on elevated ground,
which is dominated by mountains on the west.
It is on a strait three leagues long called the
Niagara River. This fort, built in 1687, of
upright stakes, was reconstructed and fortified
in 1763.' We found it constructed partly of
wood and partly of stone, well fortified on the
land side and surrounded by a moat, with bastions mounting eighteen cannon, a drawbridge,
and eighty men in garrison.

Opposite the fort, to the north and almost
at the farthest end of Lake Ontario, is a large
bay called Toronto, since called York Bay by
the English. On the shore of this bay a fort
named Toronto was built by the order of
Governor de la Joncquiere. It has since been
destroyed as useless.

The next day, April 12th, we went by land
to Fort Niagara and climbed the three mountains
west of the fort. At each summit is a platform

'The British did reconstruct the fort
after its capture in 1759. J.C.B., however,
may be referring to the improvements made by
Captain Pouchot before the siege.

insert of flat and very smooth rocks which are
a resting place for passing travelers. There
are about two leagues of mountains before the
summit. When we arrived at the top, we had to
rest for a while. Then we continued our march.
A quarter of a league north of the last
mountain are the famous falls of Niagara. Its
roar can be heard three leagues away. South of
this, we came to a newly constructed warehouse,
built for working on bateaux and canoes needed
to navigate Lake Erie.[2] The warehouse was
named Toronto.[3] The English called it Scuyler
or Sckuiler.[4] At the time of our passage, it
had a garrison of forty Canadians who were all
ship's carpenters. We remained there three
days to load up with the food, goods, and
munitions that we had to take with us to the
end of Lake Erie.

The natural curiosity of a traveler made
me want to visit Niagara Falls, of whose
unusual wonders I had heard. Three of us went
to see it. I gazed at this amazing cataract,
which is in the form of a crescent extending a
quarter of a league. The usual opinion esti-
mates its height at one hundred and eighty
feet. It is the outlet of Lake Erie, and
receives its waters, which fall into the
Niagara River or Strait, which flows into Lake
Ontario near Fort Niagara. The approach to
these falls seems inaccessible, especially on
the southern side where we were. There, a
lofty rock, covered with brush growing native
to its cliffs, is encountered. Near the falls
it is impossible to hear anyone speak, except
near at hand.

---

[2]This was little Fort Niagara, built in
1750 (PHC).

[3]This is probably the result of confusing
Toronto on Lake Ontario with a similar Indian
name (PHC).

[4]Actually, they called it Fort Schlosser
(PHC).

After we had carefully examined the falls
from above, I suggested to my two companions
that we go down on foot. They pointed out the
difficulty of the descent, there being no path
nor support. They said that it would be perilous and foolhardy to descend on the bushes,
which seemed too weak to hold up a man
depending on them. The roots could not be firm
enough, since they were only secured in the
crevices of the rock. These considerations,
though the did appear convincing, did not prevent me from satisfying my curiosity. I determined, therefore, to run the risk alone, and
immediately started to descend, intending to
test the bushes I reached while going down
backward, and not letting go one branch until I
had grasped another just as solid. It took me
an hour to reach the bottom, and not without
committing my soul to Providence, for I realized the foolhardiness of my undertaking; but I
had to finish it, as much from pride as curiosity.

Finally I reached the bottom, about twenty
toises from the foot of the falls. Although
that distance did not keep me from getting wet
from the mist, I went very near, proceeding
over a fine beach of flat rocks, which led
under the sheet of falling water. Then I
became thoroughly wet; I felt the rocks tremble
on account of the waterfall, which made me
hesitate whether to advance or turn back.
However, I reflected that this trembling must
be the same all the time, and made up my mind
to advance. After thirty steps more, I found
myself in a cavern formed of rock, in the midst
of which the flowing sheets of water through
the crevices at various heights, making rather
agreeable and pleasant cascades, if the heavy
spray resulting from the fall could be halted
for a moment. Here, I thought that I was in
the very center of the falls, because the noise
and trembling were greater. This did not keep
me from examining the cavern, which seemed to
be ten toises wine and about twenty feet high.
The depth was hardly fifteen feet. I wanted to
go through it; but couldn't go far, because of

large crevices that I was unable to cross. I had to retrace my steps, as I was thoroughly soaked and numb with cold. I hurried to go back over the path by which I had descended. I climbed back more quickly than I had climbed down. When I reached the top, I found the two men I had come with, and they wanted to ask me questions. It was useless; for I was deaf, I could not hear them. Cold and hunger made me hurry back to Toronto where, upon my arrival, I promptly changed clothes, then ate.

It was not until two hours later that I regained my hearing, and could give an account of what I had seen. I have since questioned several travelers to find out whether they knew of any one who had gone down to the falls. No one had heard of it, which did not surprise me very much, knowing that Canadians do not have sufficient curiosity to go out of their way even for something worth noticing. This indifference on their part does not mean that I consider myself the only one daring to make that hazardous trip, not that others in the future will not have the same curiosity as I. But, if this happens, the one undertaking it can confirm what I have seen and reported.

In this country, a story, that passes for truth, is told of an Iroquois Indian, who, finding his canoe caught in the upper part of the current, was unable to pull himself free of it. He was resigned; wrapped himself in his blanket; lay down in the canoe; and abandoned it to the current which, without delay, plunged him over the falls to be engulfed with his canoe, never to reappear. I have seen a tree drawn into the current, go over the falls, never to appear again. From this I came to the conclusion that there was an abyss into which everything coming down is precipitated.

About twenty paces above the falls is a small island formed on a rock around fifteen toises long and ten to twelve toises wide, covered with thickets, with a lone tree in the center. The waters of Lake Erie, which surround it are very swift, running over a shingle of flat rocks. this shingle is about four or

five feet deep, especially on the southern
side, where I examined it.

A great many dead fish are found at the
foot of the falls along the Niagara River. The
voyageurs maintain that the fish come from Lake
Erie and are drawn into the falls by the rapid-
ity of the water. I have a theory in regard to
this, which seems right to me. This is that
the fish swim up-stream rather than down; and
that, coming rather from Lake Ontario, they go
too near the falls, and are killed there. Then
they are drawn into the current and cast upon
the shore, where they are often found , merely
stunned. Surely, if they had come down from
Lake Erie, they would have been killed; and
what is more, they would have been engulfed in
the whirlpool. It is said birds flying over
the falls, in spite of themselves, are drawn in
by the force of the air. I cannot confirm this
fact, which is, however, not devoid of prob-
ability, as there is often a rainbow that might
attract bird in that direction, where, becoming
wet and stunned, they could not help falling.
If that is the case, they must be migratory
birds; for those living in the neighborhood are
used to the rainbow and the noise of the falls.
It may be thought that they know enough to keep
away from it, because they are rarely seen flying near, although numerous in these parts.

April 16th, we left the storehouse of
Toronto, in canoes and bateaux. We traveled in
the southern part of Lake Erie, which is said
to be three hundred leagues in extent, and only
a hundred leagues long. This lake is beautiful
and easy to navigate. The squalls are very
frequent and to be dreaded because of its flat
bottom, which is not more than twelve to fifteen feet long,[5] and because of the scarcity of
shelter for boats. In my time, only bateaux
and canoes were used to navigate this lake, but
since then the English have built sloops, or
small sailboats.

---

[5]The author means "deep" (HRC).

The name Lake Erie came from the savage tribe of Eries who used to live on its shores. The Iroquois have entirely wiped them out, except for a clan of this tribe, who retreated into the north, and were known by the name of the Cat tribe. The southern shore is occupied by the Iroquois. they have moved back from the lake shore, as a result of the wars waged on them by the French, to have safety and freedom for their trade.

Fish are very plentiful in this lake. Swans, bustards, ducks, herons, and wild geese[6] are also hunted there.

In the surrounding woods there are found many elk, deer, bear, and turkeys.[7] During the weeks that we were navigating this lake, we lived very well by fishing and hunting.

April 24th, we arrived almost at the foot of Lake Erie, at a place called Presque Isle.[8] It is a rather shallow bay into which we entered, and where the ground plan of the fort was laid out, after an abattis of trees had been made. This fort was built of squared timbers, with four bastions mounting twelve

---

[6]Here and elsewhere, J.C.B. uses European names to designate American birds and animals. They are usually translated literally, for exact definitions of the species referred to is difficult (PHC).

[7]Turkeys originated in eastern and western America. The first sent to France were served at the wedding of Charles IX in 1670 (JCB).

[8]It now forms the harbor of the City of Erie, Pennsylvania. The usual French form is Presqu'Isle or Presqu'isle, but it seems better to go all the way in anglicising it. It means "Peninsula" (PHC).

The advance party under Boishebert landed at Presque Isle on May 3. Mercier arrived on May 15. Marin and the rest of the troops arrived on June 3. It is unlikely that J.C.B. was with Boishebert, although he may have been with Mercier.

cannons which we had brought. The fort was
given the name of the place it was built-that
is, Presque Isle.

Scurvy broke out, because of the unwhole-
someness of the air prevailing in this place
while the trees were being felled, the ground
cleared, and the fort erected, as well as the
diet of salt meat and sea biscuits, the only
food of the detachment-which had nothing but
water to drink. This malady attacked two hundred persons, necessitating the setting up of a
hospital to keep them together and to prevent
this sickness from spreading to the remainder
of the detachment.

When I arrived at this spot, I was made
head clerk of the commissary[9] [commis du garde
magasin] for the distribution of food and
trade-goods. I was for this reason better fed
than the rest of the detachment. I ate at the
table of the commissary [garde magasin], who
was served the same food as the officers-bread,
fresh game, wine, and brandy.

The commissary was forbidden to give
bread, wine or brandy to anyone but officers
and the surgeon. The commissary gave me the
same orders. I saw with reluctance, however,
that we were reduced to letting the sick suffer
and die with nothing but medicine to help them.
Troubled by their suffering, I resolved to
break the rules, and undertook to relieve a
number of sick men, if I could not cure them.
I adopted twenty-two, asking them to promise
the utmost secrecy about the comforts that I
was going to procure for them, to which the
readily agreed. Each day I put aside bread,
wine and brandy, as well as fresh game, which
made five and a half pounds of bread a day,
allowing a quarter pound to each man; five
half-setiers and a poincon of wine, giving each
one a half-poincon; as much brandy; and eleven
pounds of fresh meat, making a half pound for

---

[9]This was the first job I had while
engaged in military service (JCB).

each person. This was less likely to be missed or noticed, as I often gave them to the Indians who were sent out hunting and scouting. I had the satisfaction of seeing my patients improve daily, and at the end of a fortnight they were quite convalescent. Four or five others were buried each day. These I should like to have given the same care; but this I could not do without risking the loss of my position.

It often occurs that those whom you help are ungrateful. It is a fault commonly found among the human race. I had proof of it on this occasion. The convalescence of my patients caused me to discontinue my aid. One of them came to me drunk—I do not know where he procured the liquor—and demanded brandy from me. It was in vain that I told him he had better go and sleep. Thereupon, the crazed fellow immediately started to berate me, and seized a hatchet[10] with which he tried to strike me on the head. I escaped the blow only by jumping back quickly. I grabbed another tomahawk, that I found within my reach, and threw it rather wildly, striking him in the thigh and making a deep wound, which was two months in healing, leaving him lame for about four months. He was the only one that I had reason to complain about, nor did I pay any more attention to him, despite the regrets he expressed, and the apologies he made.

The surroundings of Presque Isle abound in game of various species, such as elk, white-tail deer, mule deer, bear, swans, bustards, ducks, geese, turkeys, red partridges, and pigeons.

The most frequent yet unusual hunting that I have seen in this place is for turkeys, which are as amusing as they are plentiful. It is usually done in moonlight, by at least two or three persons. These birds habitually go in

---

[10]A small axe carried in a belt by travelers. The English called this axe a tomahawk (JCB).

flocks, always on an elevation, so that they
can readily take wing with a gradual flight;
perhaps in the case of surprise. Usually they
descend to the ground to drink only when night
comes. They choose the tree tops with the
branches to perch on. There, they congregate
beside each other, with as many on each branch
as it will hold. Sometimes you will find
nearly one hundred and fifty turkeys in the
same tree.

When you have located an area where the
turkeys live, you will approach silently as
near as you can to the tree where they are
perched. Without speaking or moving, the
hunter then fires his gun, usually bringing
down four or five turkeys. Those remaining do
not fail to awaken at the sound. They then
squawk and, if they hear no noise, go back to
sleep. You shoot again, and the same thing
happens until all are killed, or you find you
have enough. If it happens that some turkeys
fall, merely wounded, and run away, the hunters
ought to let them escape, because those in the
tree may otherwise become alarmed and take
flight. Thus the hunters lose more. When you
finally think you have enough, those killed are
gathered up and carried to the canoe. This was
brought as near as possible to the hunting
ground. Otherwise it would be impossible to
take many, since some of them weigh as much as
thirty-five pounds. It is only by surprising
them, that these birds are killed in daylight.
If they are surprised and pursued on the
ground, when they cannot fly because of their
weight and sufficient space, they use their
feet to an elevation with such speed that a dog
can hardly follow them. When they are high
enough, they take wing on the side toward an
open space and fly far away.

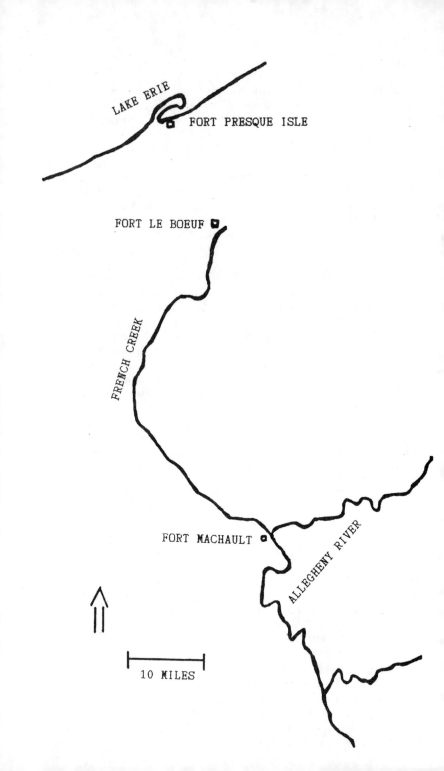

LAKE ERIE

FORT PRESQUE ISLE

FORT LE BOEUF

FRENCH CREEK

FORT MACHAULT

ALLEGHENY RIVER

10 MILES

V

*The subject of this chapter, the Pean
expedition, took place the next year, 1754.
The journey from Fort Presque Isle to Detroit
is detailed in the journal of Joseph Gaspard
Chaussegros de Lery, a marine officer who was
going to Detroit to assume the post of second-
in-command. Although J.C.B.'s geography is
generally correct, his dates are incorrect and
he fails to mention Detroit, the largest
settlement west of Montreal. According to
Lery's journal, the last section of the Pean
expedition arrived on August 12, and the whole
left for Michilimackinac on August 16.*

July 20th, when the work on the fort of
the Presque Isle was well advanced, we left
Captain Saint-Pierre there as commandant, with
one hundred and fifty men in garrison, and
departed with three hundred men in canoes to
visit the northern tribes of savages.' The
object of this voyage was to over-awe these
tribes, most of whom had seen only a few traders, and never that many Frenchmen at one time.
It was also to keep them from helping the

'July 30, 1754, a force of 285 men under
Pean left Presque Isle for a tour of the
northern posts. There is no evidence for such
a journey in 1753. Pean, Marin, and Le Mercier
held a council together at Presque Isle, August
14, 1753. St. Pierre was not commander at the
fort in July of either year (PHC).
Marin died on October 29, 1753.
Repentigny assumed temporary command until St.
Pierre arrived at the beginning of December.
St. Pierre was recalled on December 25 and
Contrecoeur was named to replace him, although
he did not arrive until March 1754.

English, who had not ceased stirring them up against the French since the year 1749.[2]

We went to the northwest, which is the most remote part of Lake Erie. Then we reached the north of the same lake and camped at Isle des Serpents a' Sonnettes, which is located at the end of the Detroit River.[3]

This island gets its name from the snakes that infest it, which we had to drive away, lest we be annoyed in our camp. Therefore we started shooting them. Several entered the hollow of an old tree. With three others, I began to fire shots into the hollow. After several shots some of the snakes rolled out like a ball of twine, many living, and some dead, cut to shreds and dragged away by the living ones. We killed several others with sticks, and cut off their rattles which, according to the voyageurs, show the age of the creature by the number of rattles at the end of the tail. Some have thirty or more, which proves how old they grow. These rattles are small round pellets, that roll freely and separately in a dry transparent skin about three inches long, depending on the age of the rep-

---

[2]English activity had started before 1749.

[3]Although there is a Rattlesnake Island in Lake Erie northwest of Put in Bay, Ohio, the statement that they were at the entrance of the Detroit River would suggest that this island was not the location of the camp. J.C.B. probably camped in the group of islands at the mouth of the present-day Huron River, north of Pointe Mouille. De Lery commanded a brigade of this expedition as far as Detroit. His journal shows the route of the expedition followed the south and west shores of Lake Erie including using Sandusky Bay. De Lery camped on Bois Blanc Island the night before the arrival in Detroit and states that Pean spent the night behind him near the "channel of the peninsula[?] and the other canoes in the islands."

tile. They are fastened lengthwise down the
middle, with two sides separated in such a way
that each pellet or rattle is enclosed in its
own compartment. These are placed parallel,
like the two ends of a chaplet, beside each
other, in a manner that when the tail ends in
one bead it shows the uneven years, and when it
ends in two beads the even years of the creature. From this, it may be seen that a new rattle is added each year. When the snake rattles
its tail, it is warning of the danger to others. It is asserted that all sorts of colic
can be cured by steeping the tail in white wine
or bouillon, and drinking it.

The rattlesnake's jaws are provided with
gums shaped like teeth, two of which are sharp
and burst open when they bite. It is the creature's venom which makes the bite dangerous.
Usually they do not bite unless they are
molested. Otherwise they flee. It is in self-
defense that they bite, for they are timid
rather than brave, and easy to kill with a
wooden stick. We killed a hundred and thirty
of them, waging a murderous war on these reptiles, who would have reason to dread travelers
for many a day.

These are various ways to cure rattlesnake
bites. The first is with an herb called
snakeroot, which is an antidote for the venom.[4]
The savages used it with success, applying it
to the skin after chewing. The voyageurs, who
do not know this herb, carry around their necks
a small bag filled with salt. When bitten by
this snake, the victim chews the salt in his
mouth. When this is mixed with saliva, he
gashes the wound with a gun flint and applies
it. The salt can thus penetrate to the venom
and prevent the injury, which it would undoubtedly cause without these precautions. This
remedy is neither as prompt nor as effective as
the first. The juice of the plantain root is

---

[4]In France the herb is called *Viperine
Virginienne* (Black snakeroot) (JCB).

DETROIT RIVER

☐ FORT

△ INDIAN VILLAGE

LAKE ERIE

also used-taking two teaspoonsful every hour.
Lastly, a tobacco leaf soaked in rum may be
applied to the wound.   The two latter remedies
are used in the south near Carolina, where
there are a great many of these reptiles.

The next day, July 21st,[5] we left the
island to continue our journey along the
Detroit River which we followed and ascended
for its length of thirty-two leagues.   We discovered the River St. Denis[6] to our left-then
Lake St. Clair, which is five leagues long.   At
its entrance, a fort called Pontchartrain had
once been constructed; the name afterwards was
changed to Fort Detroit.   Later this fort was
destroyed to move the savage fur trade farther
north.[7]   Several savage clans also withdrew
farther north when they saw the French abandon
this post.   Toward the middle of Lake St. Clair
and at its right, to the eastward is the River
a' la Tranche.[8]   Following along the lake to
the west, the Huron River[9] is reached.   On it
there is a village of the same tribe.   The
Hurons retired to this place at the time of
their war with the Iroquois.

-----

[5]The first detachment of the expedition
arrived in Detroit on August 6th.

[6]Probably River Rouge.

[7]The journal of Joseph Gaspard Chaussegros
de Lery states that the Pean expedition arrived
in Detroit August 6, 1754 and departed for
Michilimackinac on August 16.   Why J.C.B.
neglects the fort, town, mission, and Indian
villages that existed in 1754 is difficult to
understand.   Detroit was the largest community
west of Montreal.   His reference to the fort
being destroyed to move the fur trade north
probably refers to Fort St. Joseph which was
abandoned for that purpose near the end of the
previous century.   It was located north of
Detroit near present day Port Huron, Michigan.

[8]Probably the Thames River.

[9]Probably the Clinton River.

After leaving Lake St. Clair, we passed the village of savage Mississagues. Farther on, and on the same side, is the River de Bellechasse.[10] The Detroit River[11] flows through a very fair country. This is generally said to be the most beautiful terrain in Canada-nature denies it nothing. Its soil is very fertile, and productive of grain and fruits, which though wild, are good. The rivers teem with fish, and the forests have all kinds of game in abundance.

After the Detroit River, we entered Lake Huron, which we followed westward to the Saginaw River at the mouth of which there is a bay five leagues wide, extending thirty leagues inland. At the entrance of this bay, is a village of savage Outaouas, called Ottawas by the English. Ten leagues beyond the crossing of the bay[12] are two small rivers, called for some unknown reason Great Bandit and Little Bandit River.[13] Five leagues farther on is Thunder Bay,[14] from which we went on to Isle aux Bois Blanc, reaching Michillimakinac[15] August 10th. There the French have established a fort for the purpose of trading with the savages.[16]

---

[10]The Belle River.

[11]St. Clair River.

[12]The crossing was from Oak Point, through the Charity Islands to Point Lookout or Whitestone Point.

[13]Probably the Au Sable River and the Pine River.

[14]Alpena, Michigan.

[15]This spelling is as it appears in the PHC edition.

[16]Fort Michilimackinac (Mackinaw City, Michigan) was established in 1715 and served as a hub for the fur trade in the west and northwest.

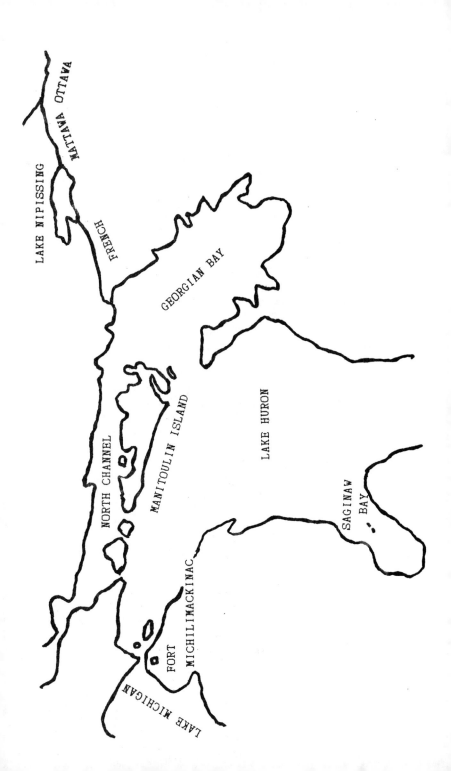

Fort Michillimakinac[17] is situated at the foot of Lake Huron. This lake is said to be three hundred and fifty leagues in circumference, and triangular in form. The fort is surrounded by a stockade, mounted with six cannon, and has thirty men in garrison who are changed every three years, if they wish. Their only remuneration is powder and lead bullets. This is enough because they cultivate maize or Indian corn,[18] and go hunting and

---

[17]This name means "Abundance of turtles." Before it on the west is Lake Huron. In the rear to the northwest is Lake Michigan, which is reached by Michillimakinac river, five leagues long. This lake is long and narrow. There was formerly, at its end, a French fort named St. Joseph, at the mouth of the river bearing the same name. North of Michillimakinac is Lake Superior, which is three hundred leagues, and which is reached by a strait twenty-five leagues long, in the middle of which is Sault Sainte-Marie. At that point there was formally a Jesuit mission among the so-called Sauteux Indians.

Lake Michigan is joined by the River des Miamis, which leads to the River Ouabache-a large river flowing northwest to enter the Mississippi (JCB). J.C.B.'s geography is confusing. The Ouabache (Wabash River) flows into the Ohio River. The River des Miamis (Maumee River) empties into Lake Erie at Toledo, Ohio. It was used as a route to the Wabash with the portage near Fort Wayne, Indiana. The route J.C.B. is describing seems to be the St. Joseph River which empties into Lake Michigan at St. Joseph, Michigan. This connects with the Kankakee River which flows to the the Illinois River and on to the Mississippi.

[18]The term corn was used for wheat in the eighteenth century. Indian corn or maize is the eighteenth century counterpart to today's corn.

fishing, thus supplying their needs. Anyone
who is contented there, and asks not to be
transferred, is permitted to remain. I saw two
men there who had stayed on, one for twenty
years, and another, a Parisian, for thirty
years. The latter was sixty years old. The
soldiers of this garrison usually trade with
the neighboring savages. It is known that
some, when transferred from this post, have
collected and taken with them, two, three, or
four bundles of pelts, which they have obtained
by trade with the savages. These they sell for
as much as ninety francs a pack-more or less,
according to the number of furs. This will
procure additional comforts for them in the
place they are garrisoning.

Michillimakinac, as I have already mentioned, is a rendezvous for all Canadians trading with the northern savages. Here is their
point of departure and their place for exchang-
ing furs. They usually leave Montreal in the
month of June, with their canoes laden with
goods. They take the northern route by the
Ottawa River, which I will speak of later.

Lake Superior flows into Lake Huron, which
has two outlets. One of them is to the west
[it is east], opposite Fort Michillimakinac
into the French River, then into the Ottawa
River, and the St. Lawrence at Montreal. The
other outlet is to the south through the
Detroit River, Lake Erie, Lake Ontario, and the
rapids, down to the St. Lawrence River. These
are the only two ways for traveling to upper
Canada. The traders prefer going by the Ottawa
River, in spite of having to make more portages, because it is a more direct route, perhaps also because of habit.[19]

---

[19]This route followed the North Channel
(north of Manitoulin Island) to Georgian Bay.
Here the traders entered the French River,
passed through Lake Nippising to the Mattawa
River which led them to the Ottawa River and on
to Montreal.

Fish are very plentiful in Lake Huron, in which are found carp, goldfish, pike, sturgeon, trout, brill whitefish, and others. The whitefish are excellent; make good soup; or can be served with various kinds of sauces. In Michillimakinac, however, they prefer them cooked in water with a little salt.

Game is likewise plentiful, for there are elk, white-tail deer, mule deer, bear, moose, beaver, otter, sable, marten, mink, weasel, fox, lynx, porcupine, turkey, wood rat, muskrat, hedgehog, turtle, etc. Later I shall tell more about the animals most in demand, and about the most remarkable hunts I was to witness in the various places I have visited.

During the twelve days that we remained in Michillimakinac, several savage tribes of the neighborhood gathered there, with whom a council was held, in three different sessions. Sixteen different tribes took part in these councils. They were: Hurons, Ottawas, Sauteux,[20] Algonquins, Potawatomies, Outgamis or Foxes, Miamis, Mississaugas, Mascoutens or the Fire Tribe, Puants, Sioux, Kickapoos, Malomines or Follavoines, Assinaboines, Pawnees, and Weas. All these various tribes differ in language as well as customs, and do not show the same degree of bravery.

Since the gathering of the savages amounted to twelve hundred men, and we were hardly a fourth of that number, we were forced to take precautions against a surprise attack, in case of any evil intentions on their part. We remained under arms, and loaded the cannons with grape shot.[21]

The first council was held under the guns of the fort. When the savages had assembled in

---

[20]French name for Ojibwa (Chippewa).

[21]Cannon ammunition which consisted of many small balls which would, when the cannon was fired, spread over a wide area. This was the equivilent of a buckshot load for a shotgun.

a half circle, the commander of the French
detachment,[22] who had presided over this council, spoke to them as follows:

"I was sent to you by your father
Ononthio,[23] to tell you he loves all his children, and wishes to give them a token of his
love by the presents that I was charged to
bring you in his name. But I am also
instructed to let him know your views about
pledging yourself to raise the hatchet,[24] and
to go with your French brothers to fight the
English. For your Father Ononthio has heard
that you have listened to evil counsel, causing
you to turn your arms against your French
brothers, who are as numerous as the leaves of
the trees. Those you see here around me, are
only a small branch of the great tree."

After the interpreters had turned this
speech into various tongues of these nations,
each chief stood and spoke, one after another.
All their speeches led to the same conclusion,
which was that they were, and always would be,
ready to march at the order of their Father
Ononthio; and also that they would levy all
their young men to go to war against the
English, who had already deceived them, and to
whom they would listen no more. The commander
replied in a few words, that he was satisfied
with their speeches, and would report their
good intentions to Ononthio; and he would give

---

[22]This could refer to Pean or the fort's
commander, Louis Lienard Sieur Beaujeu de
Villemonde.

[23]Ononthio in the Huron and Iroquois
languages means "great mountain." All the
savage tribes have adopted that word to
designate the Governor General. When they wish
to speak of the King, they call him "Great
Ononthio" (JCB).

[24]Raising the hatchet is the phrase used
by the savages to show that they are declaring
war. To do this they raise their tomahawks,
which are small axes-mentioned before (JCB).

them the presents entrusted to him by Ononthio. He had some tobacco given out, and after this distribution had been made, following their custom, they all stood up, formed a circle, and all together gave the war cry; then sat down on the ground crossing their legs in tailor fashion. They painted themselves red and black,[25] then sang the war song. Some rose and began to dance to the sound of the "Chichikoi."[26]

After this dance, they began to march in a circle following each other, calling upon Areskoui and Agrekoui[27] for aid. After they had danced in this manner the rest of the day and part of the evening, they went to bed. The French remained under arms, and did so during the whole week that the Indians stayed with them. There were two more councils held to make sure of their promises, which they confirmed by strings of beads.

In making an alliance, in declaring war or peace, strings of small glass beads of varied colors, called porcelaine in this province, are exchanged. These beads are three to four lignes[28] long, pierced lengthways, rounded and strung like a rosary in a single string. Some beads are all blue, and some of two colors mixed. The belts are made of several strings, sewn together on a band, three or four inches wide and eighteen to twenty inches long.

---

[25]They do this by dipping their fingers in the color with which they want to paint their faces in every direction, forming stripes across and down the face. This will be described with greater length at the end of these travels, in connection with their physical appearance (JCB).

[26]The "Chichikoi" is a sort of calabash filled with small stones which they shake and accompany vocally with "ugh-ugh" deep down in their throats (JCB).

[27]Savage divinities, of whom I will tell at the end of these travels (JCB).

[28]A ligne is 2.25 mm.

In an assembly, an orator never makes assertions, without giving illustrations by each string or belt, and sometimes both, that he presents. If he discusses several matters he will present a string for each one, and will take great care to remember, on any similar occasion, all that he said, and when he spoke, in regard to each string and belt. Their speeches are always as laconic as they are symbolic. they are often propounded in the assembly of the village or tribe. Each councillor holds a string or belt to serve as a reminder, when necessary, to the orator who is the spokesman. When the question of answering arises, strings and belts are given them in the same way, according to circumstances. But we always take the precaution of writing down the speeches and replies to make sure of recalling them at need.

The calumet is offered, as another sign of peace and concord. It is a good omen, when accepted. There are some tribes that present it, when they go to war. Then, instead of the calumet,[29] it is the tomahawk which they smoke in the same way. The head opposite its sharp edge is shaped like a pipe, and the handle is pierced lengthwise. It would be proof of cowardice on the part of those to whom it is presented, if they refused to smoke. They would always be despised by the warriors. When raising a war party is in question, a deputation of warriors is sent among the neighboring tribes to invite them to march. If they go by water, canoes are provided for the voyage, and if by land in winter, they make snowshoes and traines for the snow.

The *traine* is a thin plank, six to nine feet in length, and twelve to fifteen inches in width. It is bent at one end in a half circle,

---

[29]A kind of pipe made of a red stone found in the north of Canada and in the west towards Missouri. The savages present it to be smoked, as a sign of peace and friendship (JCB).

called a hood, to which a strap called a collar
is attached—made of birch withes about eighteen
feet long. The center part is about three or
four inches wide and sixteen to eighteen inches
long. This collar is used to haul a load. The
thick middle piece of the collar rests on the
forehead, or sometimes slantingly across the
chest and shoulders. The traine has, down its
length and sides sinews of animal hide into
which a cord is laced to hold the goods loaded
on the traine. Two or three hundred leagues
can be covered in this way over the snow and
ice.

Snowshoes are made in a flattened pear-
shape worked with deer sinews, and some what
like tennis raquets, but stronger, and eighteen
to twenty inches long by about fifteen inches
wide. They are fastened with straps on the
feet like skates. these are used so a man can
travel easily over the snow, without sinking
more than two inches, despite his weight. You
must take care to keep your feet apart when you
walk, and make the snowshoes pass over each
other at each step without catching, else you
will fall in the snow, from which it will be
hard to get up, especially when the snow is
heavy, and newly fallen.

During the week that the savages in council at Michillimakinac stayed there, they gave
us an exhibition of dancing an reconnoitering.
This is a pantomime showing what the savages do
on a war expedition. A man, usually a warrior,
dances alone in the midst of several who sit
around him. He begins by slowly going forward
to the center of the circle, gesturing like a
person who does not want to be seen. He
remains still for an instant, after which he
shows the warrior's departure, land march,
water voyage and encampment. Finally, pretending to reconniter and to see the enemy's
approach, he stops, looks around him, and then
suddenly going into a frenzy, starts running as
if he meant to take a prisoner, or seize hold
of a foe. In this case he shows how he breaks

his victim's head and scalps[30] him, cutting a circle with the blade of his knife. He then steps forward, puts his knife between his teeth, and appears to pull the hair off with both hands. He shows how he attaches it to his belt, while giving the death cry, of which we will speak later. Then he immediately runs away at top speed as though pursued. Such was the first act of this tragic pantomime. The savage actor, who was by then strongly agitated and wet with perspiration, had to rest.

After a short pause, he introduced the second act, beginning to run here and there, as if hiding behind trees, then standing in a listening position, and acting as though he had killed a man. Appearing to be discovered and pursued, he stopped short, to escape hurriedly in a round about way, but calling out nothing since he could take no scalp. Such was the second act. Going on with the third, the same performer began by going to war as if seated in a canoe, moving his hands and arms as if he was using an oar and changing it from one hand to the other to travel faster. Pretending to see the enemy, he beached his canoe, seemed to tie it, and then to hide in ambush to surprise his enemy. Seemingly discovered, and unable to get back to his canoe, he sought to escape through the woods. After this feint, the savage acts as if the enemy had fallen into ambush, and been killed or made prisoner. In the latter case, he shows how he takes the prisoner along in triumph, giving cries of joy. This is the last act of the pantomime.

The savages have other dances of entertainment; but as they are less interesting, no mention will be made of them.

Those savages who remained at Michillimakinac went hunting, and brought us game of several species. As they consumed a great deal of food each day, and as we needed

---

[30] I will explain later about scalping (JCB).

provisions for our detachment's trip, we
thought of sending them away. But before doing
this we had a final council. Its purpose was
to have them demonstrate again their continued
loyalty to their father Ononthio, and their
friendship for their French brothers. The savages promised it with strings of wampum, saying
they were going to march at the first word
received from Ononthio. After this promise,
tobacco, powder, balls, shirts, woolen blankets, cloth to make into mitasses,[31] pieces of

---

[31]Mitasses or mitassones, so called in the
savage language, are a kind of stockings made
of two half ells of cloth, or one ell of
milton, cut in two parts, one for each leg, and
sewed down the leg as wide as the calf, so the
leg can enter. Outside the seam a piece about
four or five inches wide is left, which flaps
freely along the leg; or the lower end may be
tucked into the shoe and fastened at the top by
a garter above the calf. When it is wished to
make this kind of stocking ornamental it is
trimmed with ribbon sewed together or in points
on the edge of the flapping outside strip. To
this ornament the savages often add porcupine
quills fashioned in various colors, as well as
animal fur dyed red. They also fasten on
little bells sold to them by the Europeans. It
is usually the women who give these luxurious
touches. The garters are also trimmed with
little bells or with small pieces of copper
three or four lignes in length, made like the
ends of shoelaces but widened to a cornet
shape. [These are tinkling cones which were
found in abundance in the archaeological
excavations at Fort Michilimackinac. They were
made of brass, not copper. This is a common
translation error. The French words for brass
and copper are identical except that copper
should be identified as red copper, a
technicality often missing from period
documents. This item was also made from other
metals. Cones of copper, pewter, and sheet

ribbon, and knives were given them. They
seemed satisfied and left the next morning.

We said before that game was plentiful in
the neighborhood of Michillimakinac, and that
we would tell of the animals most in demand by
the hunters for their hides and furs. Here are
the details:
The otter is a voracious animal living
along the shores of lakes and rivers. It usually lives on fish; that failing, it eats
herbs, bark, and water plants. Its habits have
classed it among the amphibious animals who
live on land or in water. Because it is black,
the fur of the otter in the north is more beautiful than anywhere else and consequently most
sought for.
The mink is greatly valued by the hunter.
This animal is of three species. The first is
the common mink, the second is the vison, and
the third is called the stinking beast, because
of the liquid it discharges, when pursued,
taints the air far and wide. This latter animal is pretty, and as tall as a cat, but heav-
ier. Its fur is glossy, somewhat grey, and
marked with white stripes in an oval shape from
neck to tail. The tail is bushy like that of a
fox and is held upright like that of a squirrel. The marten and the mink, as well as the
fisher and the polecat, are wild cats which
differ only as to fur. They all make war on
birds.

---

metal were found at Fort Ligonier] They are
attached so closely that they touch and make a
sound that can be heard from afar when the man
or woman wearing them is in motion. Shoes of
the savages are trimmed in the same way. They
are called moccasins or mockassons. These will
be spoken of at the end of these travels when
describing their clothing. The savages also
wear mitasses of deer or elk skin, but they do
not trim them. The men prepare them, and the
women sew them.

The rat is useful only for its skin, which is an article of commerce. There are two kinds. The wood rat (opossum) is much larger than in France, and its fur is silvery grey, sometimes white. The female wood rat has a pouch under her body which she opens or closes at will. She puts her young in it, when hunted, and thus escapes. The other species is the muskrat, so called because its testicles contain an extremely exquisite musk. It has all the favorite pursuits of the beaver, whose miniature it seems to be except for its tail. It lives, like the beaver, on the banks of brooks and small rivers. It can be seen only from the month of March until the winter's approach. During winter it takes shelter in a hole in the ground or in a hollow tree, without coming out.

There are three species of squirrels in the north: the red squirrel, which is larger and stronger than that of France; the ground squirrel, which is white and smaller than the red squirrel; and the flying squirrel, which leaps from tree to tree, a distance of forty paces. This ability comes from having a fold of skin two inches long on both sides, reaching from the forelegs to the hind legs. The Canadian squirrel is very easy to tame. It can pick out its master among several people. There are still other squirrels of a much more beautiful species, which will be spoken of later.

The weasel is the size of a squirrel, but a little shorter. It has sharp eyes, a shrewd expression, and movements so quick that the eye cannot follow them. The end of its long, thick, and very furry tail is jet black. Its fur, which is russet in summer, becomes white during the winter. This animal is one of the beauties of Canada, smaller than the marten and more rare.

The marten is found only in cold countries, in the midst of forests, far from any settlement. It is a hunter and subsists on birds. Though it is only eighteen inches long, the tracks it leaves in the snow appear to be

made by a very large animal, because it goes
only by leaps, always on two feet at a time.
The fur is much in demand, though it is not so
valuable as the sable's fur, which is particularly black and glossy.

The most beautiful species of marten is
that whose fur is a deeper brown reaching down
the back nearly to the tail, which is always
nearly black. The martens live in the thickest
part of the woods, and usually emerge only once
in two or three years. The savages upon their
appearance predict a good winter, which means
plenty of snow to bring them good hunting.

The fox is a carnivorous and destructive
animal, originally from the frozen regions, but
naturalized since then in the temperate zones,
where it has not retained its original beauty.
In the far north above Lake Superior, it has
preserved its long bushy fur, often red, and
sometimes white or silver-grey. The most beautiful and the most rare is the black fox occasionally found in the northern part of Canada,
but less often than in Muscovy which is farther
north and not so damp.

From the Canadian North they still obtain
the pelts of elk, white-tail deer, mule deer,
beaver, bear, etc. The elk, white-tail deer,
mule deer, and bear are the most common quadru-
peds of this country. There are some found
everywhere from north to south. When a deer is
young, its fur is tufted and striped white and
red. The animal is not fierce; men can easily
tame it. The tamed female at mating time goes
to the forest, and when covered returns to the
home of her master. When her time arrives to
bring forth her young, she again retires to the
forest, where she remains several days with her
little ones and then returns. If they wish to
keep her fawns, they follow her into the woods
and bring back the little ones, which she con-
tinues nourishing at the house.

The bear, which is usually black, is more
morose than ferocious. Instead of a cave he
chooses the hollows of fallen or upright trees
for his retreat, and lodges there in the winter, climbing up as high as he can. He is very

fat toward the end of autumn, and his coat is thick. Because he is inactive and sleeps almost continuously at this season, he does not lose weight from exhaustion. He rarely comes out of his winter home to hunt food, but maybe forced out either by knocking on the foot of the tree, by building a fire against it, or by felling the tree.

Three men ordinarily go to hunt bear in this way. One of them strikes the foot of a tree with an ax. The animal inside always scrambles to the top of the trunk, where he puts out his two paws, pokes out his head, and looks down to see what is happening. If he sees danger he goes back in his hollow, and the tree must be cut down to make him come out. Sometimes, however, repeated blows with an ax force him out to climb down backwards. Only if he starts down will the hunter fire a shot into his head; and if wounded, he hurries his descent and, halfway down lets himself drop. At the same instant or or two more shots are fired at him. If by chance he is not killed, and has sufficient strength left, he advances on the hunter in sight, who jumps behind a tree and takes aim. The two others then fire and, when thus attacked, the animal is usually laid low. The hunters run up, cut off his paws with an ax, and cut his throat, after which he is disemboweled.

They throw away the entrails, take off the skin, and cut off and carry away joints to be smoked and eaten. Never do they fire on a bear when he is at the top of a tree near his hollow, because he retreats into it. Then they can get him only by felling the tree and cutting it to pieces. Savages rub themselves with bear grease, especially the women, who use it on their hair. The skin is used as a mattress, and also as an article of commerce. This animal usually mates in July. During this month and the following one, it is very thin.

The beaver is another very profitable article of commerce. More will be told later of its ingenuity and of the way it is hunted.

VI

*The French decreased the garrisons of
Forts Presque Isle, Le Boeuf, and Machault,
during the winter due to the the difficulty of
supply and little danger of attack in the first
few years of their existence. Also, since most
of the manpower was provided by the militia, it
allowed these men to return home for the autumn
harvest.*

The third of September, we left
Michillimakinac in our canoes, going northeast.
At the right we left behind Manitoulin Island,
inhabited by two clans of Ottawa and Sauteax
savages. Next we entered the French River, one
of the outlets of Lake Huron. We followed this
river for forty leagues of its length. It is
very narrow in several places, and full of
falls and portages. The river derives its name
from the fact that a number of Canadian traders
on their trading voyages were several times
attacked there and robbed of their goods
(sometimes killed), by strong parties of
Iroquois who lived in these parts. The savages
would lie in ambush in the places best suited
to conceal the lurking foes, sometimes on one
side, sometimes on the other side of the river.
We saw there the remains of fortifications
built by the savages in the former days. They
were large stones piled one on top of the
other, and held together with earth four feet
high and twelve to fifteen inches thick, in the
shape of a rectangle and a half circle. But
since the Iroquois left these parts and moved
south of Lake Erie, travel on the French River
was no longer dangerous for the Frenchmen, who
traveled it freely.
　　In the course of this river is Lake
Nipissing, where there is a tribe of savages of
the same name, who are really Algonquins. This
lake is ten leagues long and is west-northwest

of the French River. After we had paddled the length of the lake, we passed a number of rapids where the travellers going up the river must make portages. These rapids are called La Marquise, Les Talons, Les Roses, L'Epine, and Les Galops. After passing the last one, we found a fork of the French and Matahouan Rivers, which join together and empty into the great river of the Ottawas.

Though this river is very large, in several places it lacks sufficient water during the summer, because the beavers dam its course for their own convenience, making portages necessary. These animals, however, make navigation less difficult for the voyageurs by halting the flow of water for a certain distance. It backs up to a considerable depth behind the dams they have built. When the voyageurs want to go through with their loaded canoes, either up or down, they have only to break the dam. The water then makes a strong current, which sometimes carries their loaded canoes as far as two leagues. Here they find another dam, and have to do the same thing, and so on, until the voyageurs find enough water without the help of dames. The dams are restored or rebuilt by the beavers when the voyageurs have gone. The construction of these dams will be explained later.

The beaver is a very docile amphibious animal. There are three kinds: the black, which is the most beautiful; the red, which is called the terrier because it is a subterranean dweller, thus spoiling its fur; and the white, found only in the far north. The largest beavers are about three feet long and sixteen inches broad. They weigh as much as sixty pounds. They are covered with two kinds of fur, except on the paws where the fur is only an inch long. On the back the fur is coarse, glossy, and two inches long; the rest of the fur is a fine down, and this is most in demand. The paws have nails. The hind ones membranes like fins. It is claimed the male lives from fifteen to twenty years, and the female not so long; the latter carrying her young four

months. The usual litter is four young ones;
actually she has but four nipples.

The beaver's muscles are extremely strong,
its intestines delicate, its bones very hard;
and two jaws-almost the same size-have extraordinary strength. Each jaw has ten teeth-two
incisors and eight molars. The head slightly
resembles a wood rat's. The muzzle is a trifle
elongated; the eyes are small; the ears short,
round, and shaggy on the outside, and hairless
on the inside. Its tail is flat and of an
elongated oval shape, fifteen to sixteen inches
long, and six to eight inches across the middle. The tail is about four inches across at
the root; two or three inches broad at the end;
and an inch and a half thick; the whole covered
with a fine blackish scale. Its flesh is white
and firm, with a strong backbone down the center.

The need to live and multiply brings these
animals together in the summer time, sometimes
fifty to a hundred, always on the river banks.
When the water is not deep enough to suit them,
they stop the water with a dam across the
river, made of pile-work twenty or thirty feet
long, six to eight feet thick at the base, and
slanting towards the top to a height of eight
to nine feet.

When the beavers undertake this work, several surround the nearest tree to the river,
and gnaw at the side towards which they want it
to fall. After the tree is down, they place
themselves five or six feet apart, and gnaw
along the trunk. Others work at its branches,
cutting them about four feet long and putting
them aside, either for eating the tender wood,
or for construction work on the dams. They cut
the branches evenly, and pile them carefully as
high as nine or ten feet, with no sticks pro-
truding. One looking at this work would say
that it was done by men rather than by animals.
As to the trunk of the tree, several will roll
or push one piece after another, placing them
where the dam is to be built across the river.
There they wedge each piece in place with
sticks and stones. When the first layer is

well secured, they begin another with the same
care, narrowing it toward the top and, as the
dam grows higher, putting on a layer of earth
mixed with brush to hold back the water after
the dam is completed.

Above the flow of the current, the industrious beavers make three tiers of holes in
which they live singly, in the lower tier
first, with their tails always in the water.
When the water floods the first tier, the beavers climb down to the second, and so on to the
last tier. When the water reaches the last
tier, the animal makes holes in the dam to keep
the water from rising higher.

The animal plans its work so wisely that,
while they work, two of them are stationed as
sentinels about a hundred paces from the job.
At the slightest noise, the sentinel whistles
to warn the workers, who hide until the sentinel reappears. This is a signal that the danger is over, whereupon each one again takes up
the task.

Even while working on the dam, beavers are
busy with their winter supplies, gathering
small tender twigs of wood and bark from such
trees as the alder, fir, wild cherry, aspen,
and poplar. Each beaver has its own particular
storehouse. They respect each other's property, from which it follows that they work
together but live alone. These colonies are
common enough along the French and Ottawa
Rivers. They are most numerous in the months
of June, July, and August, because in these
months these animals assemble for their work.
About the middle of September they begin to
mate, and in spring the female bears the young.
When weaned, they are fed on fish, crawfish,
and tender wood.

The red beavers or terriers, as I have
said before, live underground. They live apart
from the others and do not work. Therefore,
the workers chase them away and battle with
them whenever they meet. It is easy to recognize terrier beaver by the rough fur on their
backs, and because they are much thinner than
the others.

Hunting for beaver is done only in winter, and not oftener than once in two years, so that the species will not become scarce. Hunting them is not difficult, for this animal is very far from showing the same strength in defense and the same skill in avoiding the snares of its foes, that is shown by its ingenuity in building shelters, and its foresight in procuring the necessities of life.

They are hunted in four ways; by nets, by chopping, by traps, and by lying in ambush for them. They seldom use the net or the ambush, for the tiny eyes of this creature are so sharp and its ears so keen that it is hard to get near enough to shoot it before it plunges into the water, which is seldom far away. Even if wounded, it lost to the hunter if it is ready to dive in the water, because it never comes up when it dies of its wounds.

More usually the hunter resorts to chopping or trapping, because these animals are partial to a diet of tender wood, and go out in the open to look for it. The savages, being aware of this, arrange traps shaped like a figure four along their tracks, and under these traps place small pieces of fresh-cut green wood. The beaver no sooner touches this bait than a heavy log falls on its head, breaking its back. The hunter, who is in hiding, comes out and dispatches it without difficulty. The chopping method requires more care. This is the way it is done. When the ice is only four or five inches thick, a hole is made in it with an ax, and reed-grass is thrown around the edge. The beaver comes up in it to breath more readily. They can be heard from quite a distance, because the create a great commotion in the water by their breathing. When the creature has reached a hole in the ice, it puts its two forepaws on the edge, and sticks out its head. Then you knock it on the head, and seize one paw to throw it on the ice, where it is beaten to death before it recovers its senses.

If the lodge is near a stream, the hunting is even easier; for you cut through the ice and set a net, then break into the lodge. The bea-

vers inside always try to escape to the water,
and are caught in the net. They must not be
left there long or they will free themselves
very quickly by cutting the nets. When the
animal is captured, it gives a plaintive cry.
It is generally believed that the voyageurs
destroy these animals when they come to their
dams. Not at all; the benefit they derive from
the beavers is too great. They make it a rule
never to harm them when they are at work, for
without the beavers' efforts the voyageurs
would have to make frequent portages with their
canoes and merchandise, which they avoid by
opening the dam. Such is the character and
industry of the beavers, as well as the way
they are hunted.

Following the Ottawa River, we passed several rapids, such as La Roche Capitaine, the
great and little Allumettes, La Roche, Fendue,
Les Calumets, then the River Rouge, and
Chaudiere Falls. Afterwards we came to the
plains, where we camped September 12th, at
about three o'clock in the afternoon.

When we arrived at this place, we saw a
bear swimming across to our side of the river
at the distance of a rifle shot.' I was one of
four who ran forward not only to prevent his
approach but to kill him. He had no sooner
touched land than we fired three shots at him.
When he shook his head and continued to
advance, I rushed forward near enough to plunge
my hunting knife into his right flank, where
the bear's next movement forced me to leave it.
Thereupon, he immediately fell on me and held

'The reference to rifles and rifle shots
are somewhat misleading. A modern translation
dictionary will translate the French word *fusil*
as rifle. In the eighteenth century the fusil
was a smoothbore musket. A rifle shot would
be, conservatively, twice or three time the
distance of a musket shot. J.C.B. and his
fellow soldiers used muskets, therefore this
distance is conservatively, one hundred yards.

me between his two forepaws. My companions,
seeing my situation, and not daring to shoot,
could only shout to frighten him. The creature
turned me twice, right and left. At all
events, I played dead because I recalled
hearing that this was the only way to escape
the fury of such an animal. At this time, my
companions, who could not frighten him with
their shouts, decided to fire several shots in
the air. Then the animal left me, after he
held me under him for several minutes, which
seemed long enough to me. He then went
sedately to the edge of the woods, where he
turned and sat down on his haunches, looking
back at us daringly, in spite of many shots
where we were firing at him.

The rest came up to me, as soon as he had
left. I got up, and, like the others who came
up at the news of my mishap, went in pursuit of
the bear who escaped into the woods with several bullets and my hunting knife in his side.
We followed him by the traces of blood, for
about half a league, where he stopped and
received several more shots which brought him
down on his side. We immediately advanced on
him, and finished killing him. I got my knife
back, which has only entered his paunch. He
was then disemboweled and cut into pieces.
Everyone took his share to carry back to camp,
where we ate it together.

September 15th, we went from the Ottawa
River into the Lake of the Two Mountains at the
mouth of this river. We followed its length
for two leagues and then entered River des
Prairies which, as we said before, separates
Isle Jesus from the Island of Montreal.

The 17th, we stopped at Montreal, where we
stayed a week to rest from the fatigue of our
journey of nearly five hundred leagues. The
route that we had just followed from
Michillimakinac is, as I said, the one used
most commonly by the traders for their commerce
with the northern savages. They usually
require five weeks to go by this route from
Montreal to Michillimakinac with their canoes
and trade-goods.

The 25th, we left Montreal in bateaux for Quebec with only one hundred and twenty men.

October 3rd, we arrived at Quebec. I made social calls on the people I knew. As a campaign in January of the next year was already contemplated, and as I had been informed I should be included in this detachment, my only thought was to pass the short time left me in an agreeable way; so I used it for rides in carioles[2] and for society balls.

During November a messenger arrived in Quebec, sent to the Governor General by Captain St. Pierre, commander of the fort of Presque Isle, to announce that he had had a visit from an English officer, the bearer of a summons ordering the French to evacuate this post and all neutral lands, which were to be used only for trade with the savages. He had answered that he was on French territory and could not retire without orders from his general, to whom he would transmit the summons. He had been extremely polite to the English officer before sending him away.[3]

While Governor Duquesne heard of this order from the Governor of Virginia, named Dinwiddie, he also received news which informed him of the preparations being made in the English colonies to attack the French under the pretext of protecting the savages. The pretext was even more mendacious because the French treated all the savages well, and sought only to find ways to gain their friendships. But then, wishing to get into a position where force could be met with force in case of attack, he decided to send a strong detachment

---

[2]Carioles are a kind of sleigh with iron runners which only go on snow and ice (JCB).

[3]George Washington, who was the messenger referred to, reached Fort Le Boeuf on December 11, 1753, and met St. Pierre there, not at Presque Isle. This is the only reference to St. Pierre which fits, and even here the date and place are incorrect (PHC).

of troops and militia, not only to Presque
Isle, but also to the Belle or Ohio River where
he had heard that the Indians had established a
fort. Consequently, they drew up a plan for
opening the ensuing campaign.

Among my winter diversions after my return
to Quebec, I was one of four invited to a wedding which was to take place in the middle of
December, ten leagues from the city. We left
in sleighs over the snow and arrived at the
rendezvous the same day. We had five days
filled with pleasure. When the time came to
return to Quebec, there was a very lively and
agreeable lady who wished to return with us in
our carriage. Since we could not refuse without being rude, I was the first to offer her my
seat, as the sleigh could hold only four persons. I had to hire a horse, after we had
agreed not to separate on the road. But unfortunately I got a short-winded horse, which I
rode three leagues. We slept at a distance
because we had left late.

The next day, I took another horse. It
was lame, and could make but two leagues. As
we had agreed not to separate, we stayed to
amuse ourselves in this place, where we slept,
and where my two mounts were a subject for many
jests. The day following, when we had to go
on, I was given a blind horse, which was the
final blow to make the joke complete. But at
least this horse could travel, and we reached
Quebec in the evening at five o'clock. Before
separating, we took the lady back to her home.
She would not leave till we had promised to
come and dine with her the next day. Of
course, we accepted.

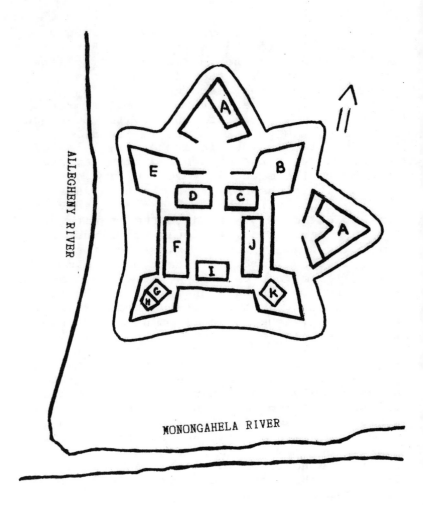

ALLEGHENY RIVER

MONONGAHELA RIVER

100 FEET

A MAGAZINE
B POWDER ROOM
C GUARD HOUSE
D COMMANDER
E KITCHEN
F OFFICERS
G CADETS
H PRISON
I STORE HOUSE
J BARRACKS
K BLACKSMITH

VII

*J.C.B. is in the party that establishes
Fort Duquesne and sees his first military
action. If he was a part of the Pean expedition (Chapter V) he must have left Fort
Duquesne after the battle at Fort Necessity.
It is possible that this happened. Captain
Mercier was at the battle of Fort Necessity and
with the Pean Expedition. Also, Lieutenant
Carqueville, according to the Lery journal, had
taken a convoy of supplies to Fort Duquesne
June 16 and returned to Fort Presque Isle July
27. This would place him at Fort Duquesne during the Fort Necessity affair. It should be
noted that the author gives no further information concerning 1754. The next chapter,
although dated 1754, discusses events of the
next year followed by general information concerning native customs. He concludes with his
return to Quebec dated 1754, but there is no
event or detail to support that date. This
could support his not being at Fort Duquesne,
but with Pean in the latter half of that year.*

Year 1754: At the beginning of January,
they raised five hundred men, as many regulars
as militia. They did not fail to include me in
this number, as I had foreseen. We left Quebec
by land, on the 15th, under the command of
Captain Contrecoeur[1] and other officers.[2] We

---

[1]Claude Pierre Pecuaudy, Sieur de
Contrecoeur (1706-1776) was Canadian-born. He
was second-in command of the Celoron expedition
in 1749 and commandant of Fort Niagara in 1752.
He was made a Chevalier de St. Louis in 1756.

[2]According to Contrecoeur's letter of
November 28, 1755, he set out from Niagara in
January, 1754 (PHC).

traveled over snow and ice all the way to
Montreal, which we reached on the 26th. We
stayed there a week while taking on reinforcements of three hundred militia, and supplies
for two months.

We left by land, February 3rd, with a
traine to each man (a sort of board which I
described before). We passed the village of
Lachine and then went over the ice to Isle
Perrot; from there to the mainland, skirting
Lake St. Louis, and St. Francois, as well as
the rapids and Lake Ontario, always going to
the northwest. We often had to cross rivers in
water where the ice was too weak to risk going
upon it. This must be done by undressing and
carrying the clothing on our heads, and after
crossing, we had to dress again very quickly
and run to warm up. This occasionally happened
three times in the course of a day. We experienced this discomfort four days of our journey.
Then we were compensated for it on the shore of
Lake Ontario, where the ice was strong enough
to hold us, and where those who could skate
pulled seven or eight traines in a row, one
after the other with men upon them. We traveled in this way for twenty leagues. Thus we
reached Toronto Bay, which has been mentioned
before. Bateaux came from Niagara beyond, and
we crossed the end of the lake by water.

February 25th, we reached Niagara, where
we left one hundred men to reinforce the garrison of this post. Then we went on by land,
climbing the three mountains near the Falls of
Niagara to reach Toronto where there were
bateaux and canoes to carry us to Presque Isle.
We stayed there three days. This gave me an
opportunity to go and see the famous Falls of
Niagara again, without intending to descend
them as I had done the previous year.

We left Toronto on the 28th in ninety
bateaux and canoes, following the south shore
of Lake Erie as far as Presque Isle, where we
arrived on March 8th. We immediately made a
portage as far as the River aux Boeufs, which
is four leagues distant from it. This portage
lasted for twelve days, because the artillery

had to be dragged. When that was accomplished,
we left two hundred more men at Presque Isle,
and we set out with only five hundred men for
the River aux Boeufs.

March 25, we left the fort of the River
aux Boeufs in bateaux and pirogues,[3] all loaded
with food and munitions. We had to navigate by
short stages on the river, because it was
obstructed by many trees which had fallen into
it, either from old age or because of the hur-
ricanes which are common enough in these parts
where whirlwinds often uproot trees. Many had
to be cut and others had to be cleared away, to
get through.

As we were making a halt one day on the
riverbank, while we were going down, we saw
several of the white-tail deer and mule deer
which abound in this country. I was one of
four who seized a gun, intending to kill at
least one. I had with me my dog;[4] a very keen
creature, full of vigor. When he found the
deer scent, he took up the chase farther than
he should have; for when it came time to
embark, I called my dog without avail. I could

---

[3]Pirogues are made of the trunks of birch
or whitewood trees from which the bark is
stripped. They are hollowed like a trough, cut
square at the stern with a sharp point at the
bow. They are rather flattened in the bottom
and underneath, but very liable to tip when a
foot is put on the side (JCB).

[4]This dog, which I had for two years, and
cost me three hundred francs, had already
earned two hundred francs by his strength and
skill. This is without counting the other
services he had done by drawing my traine over
the snow and ice (JCB).

In Peter Kalm's report of his travels in
Canada, he tells of the many chores dogs
perform, hauling water, wood, and goods for a
traveler, or even the traveler. They were
known as the poor man's horse (Kalm 1937:475-
476).

not wait for him, since I had to follow the
other pirogues. When we had finally gone about
a league down the river, I saw my dog on the
heights of the steep cliffs, from which he
could not descend to get back to me. I was
then forced to abandon him, not without much
regret, sure that he could only die of hunger
and be the food of ferocious animals.

April 4th, we reached the lower part of
River aux Boeufs, where it forks with the River
aux Iroquois.[5] They flow together into the
Ohio or Belle River, which rises in the
Iroquois country toward Lake Erie and flows on
into the Mississippi after its junction with
the Wabash River. About ten leagues below the
mouth of the River aux Boeufs, on the bank of
the Ohio, going down, we perceived an English
fort. We crossed a league above this fort to
the same side, where we mounted four cannons on
their carriages. An officer and a drummer were
sent at once to the commander of this fort with
a summons, whose terms were substantially as
follows:

"The surprise felt by the French on finding the English established on the bank of the
Ohio River, a river belonging to France. No
doubt this violation of territory has been made
only at the request of a company of traders to
favor their commerce with the savages.
Whatever the reason, the commander and his gar-

---

[5]The River aux Iroquois appears to be
French Creek above its junction with Le Boeuf
Creek (PHC). It is possible that the River aux
Boeufs mentioned here is actually French Creek
and the River aux Iroquois is the Allegheny
River. J.C.B. had left Fort Le Boeuf
(Waterford, Pennsylvania) eleven days before
which should have been suffcient time to reach
this point (Franklin, Pennsylvania). There is
a question as to why J.C.B. does not mention
the French occupation at Venango. Fort
Machault would have been under construction at
this time.

rison could retire very peaceably from it
within an hour. Otherwise, force would neces-
sarily be used to capture the garrison and
destroy the fort." The reply of the commander
(Captain Trent) was that he would yield to the
summons.[6] The capitulation was signed at once.
We took possession of the fort in which there
were only fifty men and four cannons, but no
provisions at all. We distributed enough to
the garrison to last them three days, and
destroyed the fort, which was no more than an
enclosure of upright stakes. We put their
artillery in the boats with ours, and went to
camp five leagues farther down.

The following day, we continued our journey, and arrived at an abattis[7] of trees which
aroused our suspicion. Twenty-five men were
sent ahead by land to see if they could discover anything. They reported that they had
gone as far as the bank of a river, about two
leagues from their point of departure. This
river empties into the Ohio, and on its opposite bank is a large steep mountain bordering
the river. We at once advanced as far as this
river, where we discovered a site appropriate
for settlement by the erection of a fort. At
the forks of this river and its entrance into
the Ohio, a ground plan for construction was
laid out. It was begun by felling trees and

-----

[6]Ensign Ward, acting commander of the fort
built by Captain William Trent, surrendered to
the French on April 17, 1754. Trent was not
there (PHC).

[7]Abatis was a fortification device that
would impede an attacker's approach to the wall
or curtain of a fort. A quickly constructed
abatis used the tops of trees, that were the
waste product of logs used elsewhere, placed
and entagled before the defenders position.
Abatis might be used alone to fortify a
temporary camp. This may have been what J.C.B.
saw.

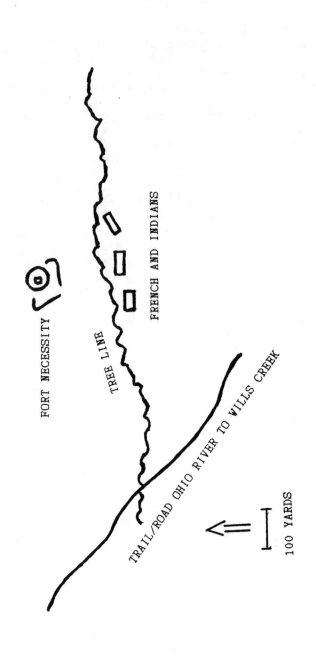

FORT NECESSITY

TREE LINE

FRENCH AND INDIANS

TRAIL/ROAD OHIO RIVER TO WILLS CREEK

100 YARDS

clearing the ground.[8]

April 8th, construction was started on this fort which we named Fort Duquesne, while we gave the name Mal Engueulee to the river which the English called Monongahela. Fort Duquesne is the most distance of the French possessions on the Ohio side, which is to the south of Upper Canada. The fort was built of squared timbers twelve feet thick on the land side; its thickness filled with earth; with a strong parapet; and three bastions each mounting four cannon. It had a deep moat on the outside and a drawbridge on the north, which is the upper side toward the Ohio.

The part of the fort next to the water is toward the west, and it is only a framework of trees driven into the ground like piles, with a bakehouse on the same side.

Inside, there are four separate buildings. The one on the right, when entering by the drawbridge, is the commander's quarters. Opposite, to the left are the guardhouse and the barracks. At the end facing the entrance is the storehouse for provisions and goods, and on the water side are the quarters of the gunners.

We worked as quickly as possible to complete the fort. It was half finished when savage Shawnees, who lived five leagues further down the banks of the Ohio, arrived there. We welcomed them, though we suspected they were spies, who must be watched. A few days later we learned that these savages had carried news to the English of our work and of our talk with them.

These savages had for neighbors another tribe called the Loups.[9] These also came to Fort Duquesne, were well received, and became

---

[8]Trent's fort was located at the forks of the Ohio, and Fort Duquesne was built on its site, beginning on April 17 or 18, 1754 (PHC).

[9]The Delaware or Lenape Indians were called Loups (wolves) by the French (PHC).

attached to the French, as the latter were kind
to these savages, who often went among the
English. As they went there freely, the French
induced them to go and see what was going on,
which they did in the most helpful and service-
able manner. They were rewarded by presents
and good treatment which, when continued,
aroused jealousy among their neighbors, the
Shawnees. They wanted to imitate them in tell-
ing what they knew about the English, and the
French profited by this jealousy. However, as
the savages are only honest as far as their own
interests are concerned, it is reasonable to
suppose that the French and English were both
being informed of what happened in each camp-
that is, in the two camps.

This spy system was dearly paid for, considering the small benefit derived from it, if
only because both sides had to be on the defensive, since they were convinced that the savages were not only deceitful but also had the
habit of exaggerating their story. This is the
reason they were told only what we wanted
known.

Fort Duquesne was almost completed when
Commander Contrecoeur sent some savages with
Frenchmen to reconnoiter. This detachment
returned at the end of several days, and
reported that the English had settled in
Virginia, forty leagues away, and were building
storehouses, probably with the intention of
attacking Fort Duquesne. Upon this news, the
commander determined to send an officer with an
escort to carry a summons to the first English
officer that he could find, but with care to be
on guard against a surprise attack from either
the English or the savages, and likewise to
encourage friendly feeling with the latter; and
especially to familiarize themselves with the
country and its various trails.

May 23rd, the bearer of this summons, who

was the sieur Dejumonville,[10] with an escort or
thirty-four men and an interpreter, departed
with the following summons:

"Word has already reached me by way of the
savages, that you have come with armed force
upon the lands of my King, my master; but I am
hardly able to believe it. Since I ought to
neglect nothing to be informed correctly about
it, I am sending Sieur Dejumonville to find
out, and in case he finds you there, he is to
summon you in the name of the king, in virtue
of orders I have received from my general, to
retire peaceably with your troops. Otherwise,
Monsieur, I shall be obliged to compel you in
all ways that I believe most efficacious for
the honor of the arms of France. The sale of
the Belle River territory by the savages gives
you such poor title that I could not be prevented from meeting force with force.

"I warn you that if any act of hostility
occurs after this summons, which is the last I
shall send you, you will have to answer for it,
since our intention is to maintain the concord
which now reigns between our two friendly
princes. Whatever your intentions may be, I am
convinced you will show M. Dejumonville all the

---

[10]He was an ensign in the troops, and had
with him another officer named Drouillon; three
cadets named Boucherville, Du Sable, and
another; with a volunteer named La Force; an
interpreter-in all thirty-five men (JCB).
J.C.B. has in other places spelled this name
Jumonville, as does Hough's translation of
Pouchot's Memoir (PHC).

Joseph Coulon de Villiers, sieur de
Jumonville (1718-1754) was born in Vercheres,
New France. He and his brothers, who also
appear in this memoir, served under their
father, Nicholas Antoine Coulan de Villiers, in
the west and in expeditions against Indians in
the Louisiana colony. Jumonville served in
Acadia during King George's War.

consideration that he deserves and send him
back at once to inform me of your intentions."

The officer Dejumonville left with the
order and summons just mentioned, and marched
until the 26th. In the evening, he had to camp
because of bad weather. He stopped in a low
ground with his escort. He was then only two
leagues from the English fort, toward which he
was directing his course.

Bad weather detained him all morning in
his camp, he was discovered by savage Iroquois,
who went at once to tell the English.
Thereupon they started out. Next morning, the
27th,[11] numbering sixty, half of them English
and half savages, they surrounded the French.
The French did not realize this until a musket
shot was fired at them by the enemy. Then
Sieur Dejumonville performed his duty by
reading the summons he was carrying. The enemy
paid no attention to it, and in a second volley
Sieur Dejumonville was killed. The rest, numbering twenty-four were taken prisoner and conducted to Winchester, which they reached on the
4th of June.

The English who defied this French detachment were led by Col. Washington,[12] who was
commander of the English fort called Necessity.
Only one man of the Jumonville party was able
to escape before or during the engagement. He
was a Canadian named Monceau, thirty-six years
old, strong and a very swift runner, who spoke
several savage tongues because he had lived on
friendly terms with them and had gone with them
on war and hunting parties, from his youth
up.[13]

This man was six days in reaching Fort
Duquesne, because he had to take a very round

---

[11]This skirmish took place on May 28, 1754
(PHC).

[12]This Washington is the same man who will
be spoken of later (JCB).

[13]Monceau is mentioned in correspondence
of Captain Contrecoeur concerning this affair.

about way. This did not prevent him, however, from running into a band of savage Iroquois, who questioned him. He told them he had just left a French party which had included some Iroquois, and that he had been sent to announce their coming. This sort or ruse succeeded very well, for they let him go, and when he was a short distance away, he took to his heels, and arrived barefoot and starving. He brought word of the defeat of the Jumonville party, but could tell only that, having gone some distance from the camp for his own duties, he heard movements, which brought him to a halt. A moment later he heard rifle shots, and close upon them, a second volley and the cries of men. Then he suspected that his party had been surprised and defeated by the enemy. This made him decide to escape and carry the news.

This report was confirmed two days later by some savages, who gave the details just described, which were repeated by an English prisoner who came several days later.

The defeat of what was a sort of embassy obliged the Commander Contrecoeur to inform Governor General Duquesne about it. The latter wrote to the Minister of Marine, who denounced it to the English Ambassador as assassination. It resulted in arousing much feeling in this country between the French and the English.

Shortly after the defeat of Sieur Jumonville, a courier arrived at Fort Duquesne bringing word from Quebec, that the King of England had sent all the governors of New England secret orders to prepare to attack Canada on all sides. This order just given was but the sequel of a previous order sent about the year 1752, as a result of misunderstandings which, originally only traders' quarrels, later became territorial disputes, and finally open war. At first it was only a secret plot to invade Canada.

June 26th, Captain De Villiers[14] commander
of Fort Chartres, a dependency of Louisiana,
arrived at Fort Duquesne with three hundred
savage Illinois, and hostages, along with several boats laden with provisions, and goods
transported by fifty Frenchmen. Upon his arrival, this officer learned of the death of sieur
Jumonville, his brother, and about the preparations in progress to avenge this death, which
was regarded as a murder. He asked for command
of the detachment which they had planned to
send under command of Sieur Lemercier who, at
the request of Sieur De Villiers, consented to
give up his place; as much to let him have
revenge for his brother, as because he was sen-
ior in rank. Sieur Lemercier was second in
command on this expedition. This detachment
was intended at first to have only one hundred
men, but was augmented by three hundred savages
who had come with Captain de Villiers. This
detachment then seemed rather strong. I was
included in it.

The 28th, we started our march up the
Monongahela River, part going by land and part
by water. We camped when we had gone four
leagues, and there held a council[15] with the
savages, during which Commander De Villiers
told of his resolution to avenge his brother's
death. It was decided that we should send
scouts ahead of us continually, and march by
short stages. Before setting out the next

---

[14]The Villiers family was large and were
very active in the war causing confusion for
historians (including J.C.B.) ever since. The
man who went to attack Washington at Fort
Necessity was Louis Coulon de Villiers. He had
arrived at Fort Duquesne from the north. His
brother, Francois, arrived from Fort de
Chartres (Prairie du Rocher, Illinois) some
time later and was active in raids into
Pennsylvania.

[15]According to Parkman, this council was
held at Fort Duquesne (PHC).

morning, mass was said at the camp by the chaplain.[16] Afterwards, we began our march. We came to a large shed,[17] built the year before and abandoned by the English later that year. This shed was forty feet long by twenty wide, made of timber laid upon each other and roofed with bark. We left our boats there with a guard of fifteen men and five savages, then continued our journey on land. We saw human footprints during the march, which made us fear we had been discovered. This caused us to redouble our precautions, not however fearing a surprise, because we still had scouts ahead of us.

About three o'clock in the afternoon, scouts informed us they had come upon a path which had not been used in three days. We supposed from this that the enemy had retreated when they heard of our advance. Yet we went on, frequently halting to wait for the scouts' reports. Meanwhile, one of the five savages left at the shed came, bringing us a prisoner who claimed to be a deserter. he was questioned at once, and told us that the English, on learning of the approach of the French, had abandoned their camp and retreated to Fort

---

[16]This man was a Recollect who had come with Captain De Villiers from Fort Chartres. This large and vigorous person had served in the cavalry in France, becoming a monk after the death of the young woman he intended to marry (JCB).

The chaplain at Fort Duquesne at this time was Father Denys Baron, P.R. There may have been a priest with either of the Villiers brothers, although Louis, who arrived with Indians, probably would have been accompanied by a Jesuit.

[17]This was the storehouse built by Captain Trent at Redstone Creek in preparation for constructing a fort at that location.

Necessity (the same as Fort de la Prairie),[18] a short distance away.

While he was being questioned, some scouts arrived and said they had seen a camp which the English had abandoned a short time before. Other scouts left immediately to go farther, and we went on marching. At seven in the evening we reached the abandoned camp[19] and stopped there. Here we found several caches of tools, whose location we changed. These caches gave us evidence of a hurried departure.

We left the next morning and marched on. About noon, we reached the place where Sieur Jumonville had been killed. Four corpses, whose scalps had been taken, were still there. They were buried and general prayers were said, after which Commander De Villiers addressed the savages upon the spot where his brother had been assassinated, about the vengeance he hoped to have with their help. They promised to back him. Thereupon the march was continued until three o'clock in the afternoon, when our scouts informed us that we were only a half a league from the English fort.

Then we advanced more cautiously, trying to get as near the fort as we could without insert being discovered. But when we sighted it, half a hundred armed men came out to engage us, probably not expecting to find us so numerous. We advanced in three columns to the right. All the savages went to the left, shouting the war cry, which so frightened the fifty leaving the fort that they turned back hastily. We advanced opposite the fort, but only within rifle shot, because the fort was built in the middle of the plain. We had scarcely arrived in this position when the fort's cannon began to fire on us with

---

[18]"Prairie" means prairie, meadow or savannah. This is doubtless an allusion to the Great Meadows, in which Fort Necessity is located (PHC).

[19]Possibly Gist's settlement.

grapeshot (they were small cannons). We were
in the woods, each behind a tree. As we had no
cannon, we could only return fire with rifle
shots. We nevertheless, reached the fort.

Our musketry-fire lasted until eight
o'clock in the evening, when we sent an officer
with a drummer to summon the commander to surrender, failing which they would be taken by
assault. Actually we had been preparing for
this by making fascines during the firing.
This precaution was unnecessary because at the
very moment when the officer bearing the summons was going toward the fort, the enemy's
flag was lowered. This was the signal that the
enemy had decided to surrender. It was soon
confirmed when the officer returned with the
decision of the fort's commander to surrender
with the honors of war. They drew up the following terms of capitulation.

"As the French have never intended to dis-
turb the peace and good will, but only to
avenge the assassination committed on the officer, De Jumonville, the bear of a summons, and
insert on his escort, and likewise to prevent
any settlement on the lands of the King of
France, we permit the English commander of Fort
Necessity to retire with his garrison and leave
the country peaceably. We promise to prevent
the French from making any insult, and to
restrain the savages with us as much as
possible. He is permitted to carry with him
all his equipment except the artillery.

"We grant the garrison all the honors of
war which are to go out with drums beating, and
with one small cannon. We are willing to treat
them in a friendly manner. Moreover, we give
our word of honor to restrain the savages, if
the commander will give his word that he will
not undertake any more settlements in the territory on this side of the mountains. As the
English have in their power an officer, two
cadets, and the other prisoners taken at the
time of the assassination of Sieur Jumonville,
they promise to send them with a protective
guard to Fort Duquesne. As security for this
promise, they shall yield at once two captains

as hostages, who will be kept until the return of the French and Canadians to Fort Duquesne. The French, on their side, guarantee an escort to return the two English captains in safety, which should be done within two months and a half counting from this day."[20]

The capitulation was drawn up and signed the same day, July fourth, the day of the attack, by the English commander, George Washington,[21] and the French officers; and the hostages were surrendered. The next morning we took possession of the fort, in which there were only twenty-five living men and twelve dead and several broken casks of rum and salt meat-in fact, a state of absolute havoc. Commander Washington left in the night with

---

[20]This is merely a summary of the capitulation, but it follows closely the version given in the *Journal of Joseph Chaussegros de Lery for 1754-1755.* The date is, however, "The third of July, one thousand seven hundred and fifty-four, at eight o'clock in the evening" (PHC).

[21]This is the same officer who gave the order to fire on Sieur Dejumonville and his escort. While escaping from the fort he forgot part of his papers, from which we learned that he had been major of militia in Virginia; and that on May 15th, 1753, he was made lieutenant-colonel of the Regiment of Virginia, at the time composed of one hundred and fifty men. His commission was received on May 30th. This man was a partisan of the savages, whom he often commanded without ever leading them to war. He was greatly loved by them, and they called him Concorins, an Iroquois name, showing their friendship for him. The same man later distinguished himself in the War of Independence of the United States of America, of which he was elected President in February, 1789, after he had, as general in chief, fought for the cause of independence from 1776 to 1783 (JCB).

part of his garrison, for he was no longer in the fort when we took possession. We went to work immediately and demolished the fort.[22] It was only a wooden building with a storehouse and a court, all enclosed by large upright stakes, and with six raised platforms for six small three-pounders, which we broke up.

We lost in this siege two Frenchmen killed and seventeen wounded. One savage was killed and two wounded.

The savages had certainly approved of the capitulation, but counted on pillage, to which we were opposed. We advised the English remaining in the fort to leave as soon as they could, while we entertained the savages. They had reason to fear the savages because one savage had been slain. The English followed our advice about the savages, but an hour after they had gone, the savages missed them, and asked where they were. When told the enemy had departed, they immediately sent a group to pursue them. They caught up with them, two leagues away in headlong flight, taking ten prisoners. They brought them to us after we had marched two leagues.

Commander De Villiers censured their conduct, which was contrary to the terms of the capitulation, and compelled the savages to take the captives back. He sent six Frenchmen along, expressly to be sure the savages carried out orders. But their agreement was only a pretense, for on the way they stripped the ten men, killed and scalped three of them, in spite of the protests of the six Frenchmen in the escort. Satisfied with their revenge, the savages started back, leaving the seven nude men in the care of the six Frenchmen. When these Frenchmen realized that they were abandoned by the savages, they let the English go, since they did not wish to be left behind, and came

----

[22]Archaeological evidence suggests that some of the pickets were pulled up to provide enough firewood to burn the rest in place.

back with the savages to us. The Frenchmen at once reported what happened, and the savages responsible were reprimanded.

July 7th, we again passed the abandoned English camp. We burned the cabins, and left the caches of tools. Here on this site, according to the report of the two hostages, a fort named Pitt was to have been built. We continued on our way, and the next day were again at the shed where we had left fifteen Frenchmen and five savages. We slept there, and burned it before leaving. We embarked in the bateaux that had been left at the storehouse. The savages went by land. We slept but two leagues away, while the savages went on at once to Fort Duquesne, which we reached the next afternoon at one o'clock. There we were surprised to find six prisoners that some of our savages had taken after the capitulation, from the garrison of Fort Necessity. They were taken to the fort without our knowledge, and there received the "bastonnade."[23] Afterwards, the savages had given two of the prisoners to the commander of the fort, who tried to buy the other four, but was refused by the savages.

---

[23]The way the savages give the "bastonnade," will be explained later (JCB).

VIII

A few days later a courier sent from
Quebec brought us news that Acadia had been
occupied by an English army of fifteen hundred
men, commanded by Generals Lawrence[1] and
Moncton. On their arrival on May 15, 1754,
they had sent out a proclamation charging the
Acadians to bring their arms into camp. At
once all the inhabitants had recanted their
oaths of allegiance and fled to Quebec, along
with the savage Abenaquis[2] of that country, but
this emigration began only after the bombardment of Forts Beausejour and Gaspareaux, previously mentioned, which occurred the 16th and
17th of June.[3]

Acadia, called Nova Scotia by the English,
is situated to the south of the St. Lawrence

---

[1]Lawrence was governor of Acadia.

[2]The Abenaquis were formally known as
Souriquois, then as Micmacs, and finally as
Abenaquis. This tribe is usually mild in
disposition and is very loyal to the French.
They are first to whom the Gospel was preached,
and among them it has made most progress.
After them come the Hurons also attached to the
French. These two tribes have produced no
saints, unlike the Iroquois who are the only
ones to celebrate saints' days. The Abenaquis
are divided into several tribes of which we
will tell at the end of these travels (JCB).

[3]The capture of Forts Beausejour and
Gaspareaux did not take place until the month
of June, 1755, and the dispersion of the
Acadians occurred in the following September
(HRC).

The surrender of these forts, after a
token resistance, caused the officers involved
to face a court-martial. They were acquitted.

River, twenty-five leagues from the coast of
Gaspe. It extends for two hundred and fifty
miles of coastline, from the borders of New
England to the southern bank of the St.
Lawrence River. The French began to settle
there in 1618. Triangular in shape, it
includes several bays and islands, such as Isle
St. Jean and others. Chibouctou, formally a
French settlement, was yielded to the English,
who became its owners by the treaty of Aix-la-
Chapelle on October 18, 1748, and named this
city Halifax.[4]

The Isle St. Jean, like Acadia situated
south of the St. Lawrence River, is twenty-two
leagues long by one league wide.[5] Its natural
curve comes to a point on each end, and makes
it crescent-shaped. Formerly, there were a
large number of obnoxious insects on this
island. Along the coast, however, it is very
healthy. It has an excellent seaport and other
commodious harbors.

The country is level and has beautiful
meadows. The soil is easily cultivated. There
is much game, wild beasts, and the better kinds
of fish. Codfish are plentiful. The population of Abenaquis[6] has always been rather considerable there, greater than in the
neighboring islands.

Its principal port, called Port Lajoie,
was later called Charlottetown by the English.
It is the chief town of the colony.

The first naval hostilities were begun on
the 17th of June in the same year, 1754, by
Admiral Boscawen against two French vessels-the

---

[4]A strange confusion prevails in this
passage. See Bouchett's map for the
description, and distances between places.
Acadia was ceded to the English by the Treaty
of Utrecht in 1713. Halifax was founded by the
English in 1749 (HRC).

[5]The width is not uniform. It is several
leagues wide at the widest part (HRC).

[6]Read "Micmacs" (HRC).

Alcide commanded by Captain Hocquard, and the
Lys commanded by Captain de Lorgerie. These
two vessels were captured in this combat, which
continued for two days.[7]

In the months of July and August, various
bands of savages passed Fort Duquesne, on their
way to make raids on the English settlements in
Virginia, Pennsylvania, and North Carolina,
which is farthest from Fort Duquesne. Newly
arrived savages, numbering two hundred, also
set out on a raid, and returned fifteen days
later with twenty-one scalps and nine prisoners. Three of these were given to the commander, and the rest taken by the savages to
their villages. There were a great many prisoners and scalps taken in all the different
raids.

This is the way the savages take a scalp
and give prisoners the "bastonnade."

When a war party has captured one or more
prisoners that cannot be taken away, it is the
usual custom to kill them by breaking their
heads with the blow of a tomahawk (a small axe,
described before). When he has struck two or
three blows, the savage quickly seizes his
knife, and makes an incision around the hair
from the upper part of the forehead to the back
of the neck. Then he puts his foot on the
shoulder of the victim, whom he has turned over
face down, and pulls the hair off with both
hands, from back to front, just as described
before in connection with the scout dance.
This hasty operation is no sooner finished than
the savage fastens the scalp to his belt and
goes on his way. This method is only used when
the prisoner cannot follow his captor; or when
the Indian is pursued. Then he wants to take
away proof of his valor. He quickly takes the
scalp, gives the deathcry,[8] and flees at top

---

[7]This happened in 1755.
[8]A short deathcry means a victory. If it
is slow and long drawn out, it is a sign of

speed. Savages always announce their valor by a deathcry, when they have taken a scalp. The English call it scalping.

When a savage has taken a scalp and is not afraid he is being pursued, he stops and scrapes the skin to remove the blood and fibres on it. He makes a hoop of green wood, stretches the skin over it like a tambourine, and puts it in the sun to dry a little. The skin is painted red, and the hair on the outside is combed. When prepared, the scalp is fastened to the end of a long stick, and carried on his shoulder in triumph to the village or place he wants to put it. But as he nears each place on his way, he gives as many cries as he has scalps to announce his arrival and show his bravery. Sometimes, as many as fifteen scalps are fastened on the same stick. When there are too many for one stick, they decorate several sticks with the scalps.

The French and the English were accustomed to pay for the scalps, to the amount of thirty francs' worth of trade goods. Their purpose was then to encourage the savages to take as many scalps as they could, and to know the number of the foe who had fallen. This precaution gave rise to a trick among the savages, either native or suggested to them. To increase the compensation for the scalps, they got the idea of making them of horsehide, which they prepared the same way as human scalps. The discovery of this fraud was the reason they were more carefully inspected before a payment was made. Consequently, the French and English finished by giving only a trifling amount in the form of presents.

---

loss. Several cries, following each other quickly, mean prisoners and scalps. If the same cries are repeated slowly, they are counted, as they give the number of men lost; and then the Indians return with their faces daubed with black (JCB).

It is shameful for the human race to use such barbarous methods. Yet, to tell the truth, the idea belongs only to the savages, who were using it before they heard of civilized nations. This horrible custom was practiced by these savages alone, and sprang from their own barbarism, for it seems never to have existed in any other nation, not even among nations who, like them, have never received any idea of civilized life.

The practice of "bastonnade" is just as ancient. When a party has taken prisoners, they take care of them and do not mistreat them. But if this party, on its return from war, passes any villages, which usually happens from pride or vanity, they take care to announce themselves at some distance from the village by cries quickly repeated. Then the young men come to meet them. When they have joined them, they lay hold of the prisoners, and force them to go between two lines formed by the young savages. They make the prisoners run to the end of the row by striking them with sticks and stones, and with their fists. The prisoner so unfortunate as to fall in the course of the bastonnade must get up quickly and keep on, or he will be beaten to death on the spot. No one is allowed to touch the prisoner when they reach the village of their captors. They then enter in the custody of those bringing them. They could not take offense at the painful reception their prisoners received, even when some are crippled by it. This sometimes happens, especially when the party has passed several villages in a few days, and the prisoners have had this treatment in each place. This disagreeable ceremony is, however, sport for the young savages.

Generally, savages have scruples about molesting a woman prisoner, and look upon it as a crime, even when she gives her consent; but when she is free, nothing she will permit is forbidden.

September 4th, I left Fort Duquesne with forty others to return to Quebec. We took the usual route by Presque Isle, Lake Erie,

Niagara, Lake Ontario, the rapids, and the cities of Montreal and Three Rivers. At last we arrived in Quebec on the 26th of October, still in canoes and bateaux. I spent three months there as agreeably as the preceding winter.

IX

This is the year of the Battle on the Monongahela, or Braddock's defeat, which J.C.B. places in the next year. The journey to Fort Duquesne is not unique, nor is the activity of the Indians raiding from Fort Duquesne. It is possible that the author was confused and used this chapter to solve a problem of chronology, or it is, like the Pean expedition, a reversal of years. The marriage of the girl prisoner, Rachile, that the author mentions in this chapter, does not appear in the records of the fort's chaplain. Elsewhere, the main French forces, under Baron Dieskau are defeated at the Battle of Lake George.

Year 1755: During January, they planned at Quebec to send another reinforcement to the upper country. Six hundred regular and militia therefore were equipped. I was one of these soldiers.

It was extremely cold on the first day of February when we departed by land with traines. We reached Three Rivers on the 6th of February, and went on from there to Montreal, where we arrived on the 13th. There we received a reinforcement of two hundred militia and left on the 17th, with traines and some men on snowshoes. We skirted the rapids and reached Fort Frontenac on the 5th of March. There we took bateaux, which carried us down the south shore of Lake Ontario as far as Fort Niagara, where we landed on the 15th.

The next day we left on land to go to the post at Toronto. From there we departed, on the 19th, in bateaux and canoes. We followed the south shore of Lake Erie to the fort of the Presque Isle, which we reached on the 27th. There we left three hundred men, and then marched on foot to the fort of the River aux Boeufs. Here we reached on April 8th. Two days later, we sent back the empty canoes and pirogues, two men to each one, to fetch the provisions left behind because there were not enough boats.

At that time, there were at Fort Duquesne many savages of different tribes, who had come expressly to war against the English. They formed five divisions, and went separately to attack the English settlements. Twelve days later, two of these divisions returned to the fort, with only one prisoner and five scalps. Three other divisions came back successively with only nineteen scalps among them. Other parties went out on raids, burned settlements, and brought back twenty-seven scalps, but not a single prisoner.

In the first days of May, sixty Ottawa savages arrived from the north. After three days' rest, they started for Virginia, and came back seventeen days later with twenty-five prisoners and thirty scalps. They burned an entire settlement of fifty-five families, the rest of whom had perished in the flames. This is how it happened. These families had joined together for greater security in an enclosure made of upright stakes, which took in all the neighboring houses of the settlement or village. Here all these families thought themselves sheltered from surprise attacks during the night. For three days, the savages spied on the men of this settlement working daily in their fields, unaware of being watched. At the end of three days, the savages, taking advantage of the fourth night's darkness, carried brush to the foot of the enclosure and set fire to it. The fire spread to the houses built of wood.

The savages watched, and did not have long to wait. The spread of the fire forced out the inhabitants. Men, women, and children, all fled for safety. But the savages, who had expected this flight, shot all who tried at great risk to escape. The fury of the savages did not abate until they were finally sated with killing. Then they took twenty-five prisoners, all that were left of the hundred and

forty individuals of both sexes who made up
this settlement. Very few escaped, according
to the report of the prisoners, who received
the usual bastonnade when the arrived at the
fort. Ten prisoners were given to the commander, who tried to buy the others, but the
savages would not sell them.

One of the ten prisoners handed over was a
young girl named Rachile. This very pretty
girl, born in Virginia of poor parents, was
captured with her aunt. She had come six
leagues to see her relative, out of friendship,
and had been at her aunt's home for a week when
the savages seized them during the burning of
the settlement. The niece and her aunt were
both in the hands of their foes, but in the
evening of the first day's march, when the
young girl no longer saw her aunt, she thought
the older woman must have been killed. In
reality, since the aunt could not walk as fast
as the savages wanted, they decided to kill her
and did so. Young Rachile had reasoned this
out when she did not see her aunt again after
the first day's march, because she knew her to
be a poor walker.

This girl, like the others, received the
bastonnade when she reached the fort, and
almost lost an eye from the blows she suffered.
Fortunately she was one of those prisoners
given to the commander as a present, and she
was cared for by the surgeon. It took her a
month to recover, and then for two months she
was overcome with fear and trembling every time
she saw a savage, and that was very often.
Rachile easily learned French. As she was
lovely, sweet, and affable, she won without
effort the heart of a Canadian who, wishing to
make her his wife, asked the commander's consent. The officer offered no obstacles, save
to specify that she must be taught the Catholic
religion. When the chaplain of the fort, who
was entrusted with this duty, believed her to
be in a state of grace, the commander allowed
the marriage to take place immediately. But
this union was disturbed a short time later

without actually being destroyed. An unforeseen incident troubled their peace.

Some savages who had taken part in giving young Rachile the bastonnade came back to go to war, and recognized her. They wanted to seize her and take her to their village, still regarding her as their slave. Her Canadian husband, becoming aware of the intentions of these savages, and fearing that they might take her by surprise and even use violence, decided to inform the commander. The latter sent word to the young savages that the young woman they wanted had been bought by him, was no longer a slave, and with his consent had married a Frenchman. They answered, "If what you say is true, we scorn the Frenchman who was cowardly enough to ally himself with his enemy."

The commander saw the obstinacy of these savages, who would willing have sacrificed the husband to have the woman, as his death would make his wife their slave; and this officer realized that libertinism was the savages' only motive. The commander saw no better was to save the young couple from their enemies than to send them in disguise at night by boat with provisions and two guides who would take them to Louisiana. This plan was kept secret for a week after it was carried out. Then the officer sent word to the savages that their conduct had forced him to send the young couple to Ononthio. There is no doubt this wise precaution kept these two people out of otherwise inevitable trouble. Three months later, news came of their safe arrival and settlement at New Orleans, capital of Louisiana. They had been well received there, because of the passport and letter of recommendation given them when they departed.

As the sixty savage Ottawas we have just mentioned had lost two of their men on the expedition to Virginia, they held council among themselves, and resolved to avenge their comrades' death by adopting two prisoners to replace the two savage dead, burning two other prisoners, and sending the remainder of the whites to Ottawa villages.

This judgment was executed the next day against the two prisoners condemned to be burned. The savages wanted to have the execution take place in front of the fort. The commander would not permit it there, though he did not succeed in buying the two unfortunate victims. Their executioners took them to the opposite bank of the Ohio, in sight of the fort. On that side many savages, with woman and children, had gathered and built huge fires to make live coals. When the two victims had to come to the place of sacrifice, each was tied to a sapling whose top was bent down, with their hands fastened behind their backs. Burning coals were thrown at their feet, but beyond their reach. Only the weight of the men kept the elastic tops of the saplings from straightening up, and the men bobbed up and down.

During this atrocity, of which only savages seem capable, the victims were surrounded by the tormentors, who sang and urged them to defy death. This suffering was yet only the prelude to greater torment which would make humanity shudder, and is reported only to show the barbarity of the savages. Yet it is a proven fact that men do not always invent and carry out the most cruel tortures. This task is very often left to the squaws, as they are thought more ingenious and subtle in inventing tortures. They use every possible effort to please their warriors in this way. This was apparent on this occasion when the squaws showed their deliberate cruelty by heating rifle ramrods red-hot, and pushing them into the tortured captives' nostrils and ears. Before this, they burned various parts of the body with firebrands. The children, for their part, shot arrows into the thighs and arms of the victims, after an interval of a few moments. The savage women came back and burned their victim's fingertips in pipes full of tobacco, then cut off their noses and ears. I must stop here and not bring to light all the atrocious things that the most barbarous of imaginations could invent. I wish only to say that all the cries, groans, and oaths uttered during these tortures only aroused the mirth of the executioners.

In the midst of these tortures, the two men were suddenly set free from their bonds as a result of their struggles; and at once, with the courage of despair, both ran to jump in the river. Whatever their hopes, they were never realized, as the savages dived after them, caught them, and brought them back to their torture place. Here, strength and courage gone, the two victims fell to the ground. Then the savages, men, women, and children, threw burning wood on their bodies, soon covering them and reducing them to ashes. Thus ended this barbarous execution.

This was not the only sacrifice by the savages which happened in our very presence. Here is another which occurred a week later, but in a different way.

A party of Illinois savages fought against the savage Mohawks, a tribe of the Iroquois nation, took one prisoner, and condemned him to be burned. This is the way it was done.

The victim was fastened, as if crucified, over a piece of green wood bent in a circle and placed flat on four forked sticks driven in the ground, the whole being two or three feet high. When the victim's body was in this position, a great quantity of live coals were thrown under him, to roast him over a slow fire. To show his bravery, the Mohawk began to sing, daring his tormentors to do their worst. This bravado seemed more the result of rage than of courage. It did not fail to arouse his tormentors, and the more courage he showed, the more fury was shown by his tormentors. At last he died cursing his executioners to the very end.
Sometimes savages manifest regret at having killed a courageous man, because they consider him brave. This is the meaning of the victim's song.

"I am brave and fearless; I do not fear death. Those who fear it are cowards. They are less than women. Life and death are nothing to the man with courage. May despair and rage choke my enemies. May I not devour them and drink their blood to the last drop. I have done so many brave deeds. I have killed so many men! All my enemies are dogs! If I find any of them in the land of spirits, I will make war on them. Now I lament my body; I am coming to death like a brave."

A savage going to his death would not be considered brave if he displayed any feelings under his tortures. This would be a sign of weakness, for which they would scorn him.

In general, savages show feelings only for warriors killed in battle, and for the death of their nearest relatives. Of this more will be said at the end of these travels, when their funerals will be described. The warriors killed are often replaced by prisoners they have taken. They adopt them, and give them the name and dignities of the dead man, with the same honors. But the one adopted must be prudent and wise in his conduct, if he wants to make himself as well liked as the man he is replacing. This seldom fails to occur, because he is continually reminded of the dead man's conduct and good deeds.

In the course of the month of June, a convoy of two hundred men in fifty canoes laden with provisions and merchandise arrived at Fort Duquesne. Among this number, there were five canoes loaded for the account of a trader with whom I was associated. The five canoes carried trade goods for the savages, as well as wine, liquor, brandy, and smoking tobacco. As soon as the canoes were unloaded they were sent back empty, with two men paddling each canoe, to the River aux Boeufs from which they had come.

A few days after the arrival of the convoy just mentioned, a courier came from Quebec bringing word that the English colonel Braddock had been made in turn a major, then, a general of all troops in America. He had arrived from Europe at Williamsburg in Virginia last February, and had selected Alexandria as gen-

eral headquarters.[1] He had formed a camp of
American troops there to which were added the
troops that had come from Europe. This account
was confirmed shortly afterward by deserters
and prisoners, whose stories all agreed. This
news caused uneasiness, as Fort Duquesne was
only forty-eight leagues from Virginia. It is
true that these forty leagues are worth twice
that distance, for the Appalachian Mountains[2]
are an obstacle which the enemy could overcome
only by opening a road for the passage of their
artillery across mountains full of rocks. This
could not be accomplished in one campaign.
This obstacle made us feel safer during the
year at Fort Duquesne. However, not a little
preparation was made for defense in the
upcoming campaign. While waiting, we sent out
parties of savages, one after another, to harry
the enemy and to keep us informed of their work
in the mountains.

The scouts brought in prisoners from time
to time. These prisoners reported the enemy's
position, as well as their slow and laborious
march. We did not always believe their
accounts; and when they were suspected of
falsehood, because they contradicted each
other, threats were used which got the truth,
as confirmed by later reports. During these
raids on the English settlements, the commander
of Fort Duquesne sent out to the northern
tribes, to induce them to come to the French
and make war on the English, who were coming to
invade the French possessions, and then those
of the savage tribes. If they loved their
father Ononthio, they would come in the spring-

---

[1]Major General Edward Braddock reached
Williamsburg at the end of February, 1755, and
established a camp at Alexandria (PHC).

[2]These mountains separate New England, now
the United States, from Canada. The English
called them the Alleghenies. The Ohio River is
southwest of these mountains (JCB).

time to aid their French brothers to fight and
drive out the common enemy.

On his side, General Braddock held a council when he arrived in Williamsburg,[3] and
decided to enlist the five Iroquois tribes to
take up arms against the French and capture
prisoners in the neighborhood of their forts.
It was easier for the English to have these
savages on their side, because the five
Iroquois nations lived in their vicinity. On
the other hand, the foresight of the French
with regard to the other nations assured that
they would always have them ready to oppose the
enemy, especially at Fort Duquesne, the point
nearest the enemy and, consequently, the most
threatened.

In General Braddock's council it was also
decided that a corps of fourteen hundred men
under the command of General Johnson[4] should go
to seize the Fort of Point a la Chevelure,
which they called Fort Frederick.[5] This was
located between Lake Champlain and Lake Saint
Sacrement,[6] south of Montreal toward the Hudson
River valley. Colonel Shirley with his own
regiment and Pepperel's was given the task of
attacking and capturing Niagara on Lake
Ontario. He was equipped with artillery for
this purpose, and in the case of retreat he was
to go to Chouguen or Oswego. There remained
the expedition to Fort Duquesne, which Braddock
reserved for himself to carry out with three
thousand fighting men. Consequently, it was
decided that he would leave Williamsburg the

---

[3]This council included most of the
colonial governors, including Dinwiddie of
Virginia, Morris of Pennsylvania, Shirley of
Massachusetts, Dobbs of North Carolina, Sharpe
of Maryland, and DeLancey of New York (PHC).
[4]Sir William Johnson.
[5]The French called this Fort St. Frederic.
The English called the site Crown Point and in
1759 built a fort with the same name.
[6]Lake George (PHC).

twentieth of the following April, and go with his army to Fredericktown.[7] From there he would reach, in the early part of May, the Appalachian or Allegheny Mountains and carry out his plan against Fort Duquesne. Then he would go up the Ohio River to join Shirley at Niagara.

Such was the plan contemplated to secure upper Canada for the English. But this plan could not be carried out as far as General Braddock was concerned. It had been delayed by the difficulty of making roads over the mountains, as has been said before. This particular difficulty caused a postponement of the expeditions to Fort Duquesne and Niagara until the following campaign.[8]

Twelve hundred troops of the line[9] reached Quebec from France under the command of Baron de Dieskau,[10] a Swiss. After resting several

---

[7]Braddock divided his army with the 48th regiment (Dunbar's) to march north of the Potomac through Frederick, Maryland and the 44th regiment (Halkett's) to the south of the river. They rejoined at Fort Cumberland (Cumberland, Maryland) in the latter half of May.

[8]Braddock's expedition was not postponed. The delay in declaring war may have caused J.C.B. to place this expedition in the wrong year, 1756 (PHC).

[9]These were soldiers of the regular army, not to be confused with the colony troops, to which J.C.B. belonged, who were part of the Ministry of the Marine. The regiments which landed in 1755 were Bearn, Guyenne, Languedoc, and La Reine. They would be joined by Berry, Royal Rouissillon, and La Sarre. The regiments of Artois, Bourgogne, and Cambis were sent to Louisbourg.

[10]In the original this name is written "Baron Dieskau" and "Baron de Dieskau" in different places, as shown in the translation (PHC).

days, these troops began their march with Baron de Dieskau. They were able to reach the Fort of Point a la Chevelure, which was threatened by an army of twenty-four hundred men under the command of the General Johnson who was mentioned before.[11]

When the French army arrived at Fort of Point a la Chevelure, they heard that the English army was advancing to fight them. Baron Dieskau held a council in which he was advised to fight in the savage way-that is, to put each man behind a tree. He rejected this idea because it was contrary to the European method. He soon realized his mistake. The English army came from Fort George,[12] situated six leagues farther at the mouth of Lake Saint Sacrement, called Lake George by the English. Baron Dieskau with his army advanced and lined his men up for battle when he discovered the presence of the enemy. At the same time the enemy, with many Iroquois savages among them, went into ambush behind trees. The action started. The French began a running fire which could not harm the enemy much. The enemy made all there shots count, doing a great deal of damage in this way. The French army was, in the end, partially destroyed, and the remainder taken prisoners of war. Their general, who was wounded in the battle, was conducted to New York, from whence he was sent to France after he had recovered.

The news of the French defeat in this engagement caused gloom in Canada, where they had much faith in the help sent them from France. This loss, however, had to be made good by raising a new levy of men and fortify-

---

[11]Johnson had about 2500 men on the Crown Point expedition, while Dieskau had 3573 men (PHC).

[12]Fort William Henry was built there after the battle. This was captured and destroyed in 1757. Fort George was built near its site in 1759 (PHC).

ing the various posts and garrisons. But following the defeat of Baron Dieskau, the enemy
took Fort of Point a la Chevelure and destroyed
it.[13] It was our most significant fort, and
might be called the key to that country. True,
there were still some small forts behind it;
but they were not in condition to withstand a
siege.

Another misfortune occurred after this
disaster. A powder magazine near the town of
Three Rivers blew up, and caused the loss of
forty persons, together with eighty barrels of
powder.

Fort Duquesne had nothing to fear during
the rest of the campaign. We continued to send
out scouts who reported that the enemy was not
advancing rapidly in their work on the roads.
The fort was then forty leagues away from the
enemy's army, and sixty leagues from North
Carolina, and ninety leagues from Pennsylvania
and New Jersey.

Yet we are still only to the month of
August. It is usually in this month that many
swimming squirrels are seen. I have already
told of the northern squirrels, but they are
not nearly so beautiful as those along the
Ohio. In the vicinity of Fort Duquesne they
are as large as rats, and have four varieties:
black squirrels, silver squirrels, ground
squirrels, and flying squirrels. The last two
do not differ from those in the north; I need
not describe them again. As regards the first
two, the black squirrel and the silver squirrel, the pelts make very beautiful furs and
their flesh is very good to eat. They are subject to itchings on their heads, particularly
during July and August. This makes them take
to the water, as many as seven or eight hundred
at a time, two and perhaps three times a day to
cool themselves. This induced me to join three
others and hunt squirrels in the river about

---

[13]Johnson did not advance and capture
Crown Point (PHC).

two rifle shots from the fort, waiting to kill
them when they came to shore.

Scarcely had we entered the woods than we
were greeted with three rifle shots. One hit a
member of our party in the shoulder, and gave
him a slight wound. When we realized that we
had three savages to contend with, we decided
to make a stand, each of us behind a tree.
After we had exchanged several shots, two of
the men, overcome by fear, left us and dived
into the water, trying to reach the fort.
Seeing that we were now only two against three,
we decided also to plunge into the water, that
we might not become the victims of too much
recklessness in an unequal fight. We were following the river's current when the three savages advanced toward us, firing at us once, and
jumped into the river to catch us.
Fortunately, when the rifle shots were heard at
the fort, several armed men came running toward
the place where they had heard the shots. When
they saw several men swimming, and recognized
the three savages by their heads, they fired on
them. The enemy had to cross to the other side
of the river, where they thought they would
find greater safety. But some Frenchmen,
cutting wood there, prepared themselves when
they saw the savages coming to the shore, and,
when they approached very close, shot and
killed two of them. The third savage, who had
a hip broken, was put to death, but first he
was questioned about his comrades and himself.
He said they were three Iroquois of the Seneca
tribe.

Such was the end of these three savages,
who would not have spared us, if they had the
upper hand. This occurrence deprived us, at
least for the time being, of the squirrel hunting we had expected to enjoy. A week later
several of us went back together with greater
caution. From this hunt we got a supply of
about two hundred squirrels. We had to throw
the heads away because they had worms in their
brains, which caused them to blacken and make
the animal somewhat crazy.

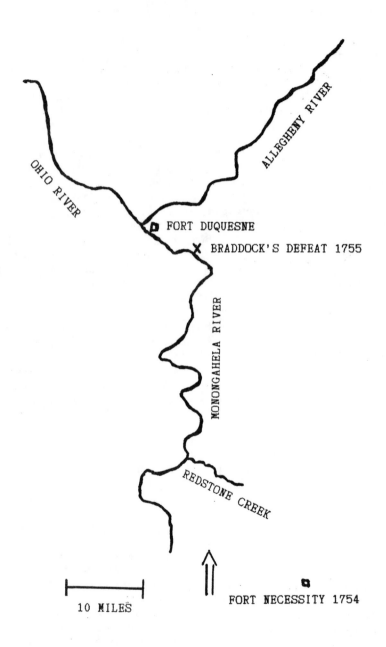

ALLEGHENY RIVER

OHIO RIVER

□ FORT DUQUESNE

✕ BRADDOCK'S DEFEAT 1755

MONONGAHELA RIVER

REDSTONE CREEK

10 MILES

FORT NECESSITY 1754

X

This chapter is J.C.B.'s account of Braddock's defeat. Again, please note, this is not the correct year. During this year, Captain Jean Dumas, the commander in the Ohio country, was sending raiding parties to the east in an effort to keep the English, regrouping after the defeat of Braddock, from mounting another expedition against Fort Duquesne. Montcalm, with the regular French forces, captured the English forts at the mouth of the Oswego River on Lake Ontario.

Year 1756: In the spring of this year there arrive in Quebec, from France, three thousand men, troops of the line, made up of the regiments of La Sarre, Berry, Bearn, Languedoc, and Roussillon, with two battalions in each regiment.[1] The whole force was led by Marquis de Montcalm, lieutenant general and commander in chief; Chevalier de Levis, major general; Chevalier de Bourlamarque, brigade commander; de Bougainville, aid-de-camp; and others, among them engineers, whose chief was Desaudrouins.

General Montcalm made plans with Governor de Vaudreuil, who had succeeded Governor Duquesne the previous year.[2] After he had

---

[1]About 1200 men, of La Sarre and Roussillon regiments, came with Montcalm. The rest had come with Dieskau the year before (PHC). The Berry regiment was initially assigned to Louisbourg and, when the English campaign of 1757 failed to threaten that place, they were sent to Montcalm.

[2]These men agreed on very little and this rivalry extended throughout the officer corps

secured the necessary information about the conditions of the defenses, he made plans for attack and fortification.

At the beginning of May a convoy of sixty canoes laden with provisions and merchandise arrived at Fort Duquesne with two hundred militia to reinforce the garrison of the fort. We learned at this time, from the prisoners taken by the savages, that Braddock's army had left Fredericton and had reached Fort Cumberland in Virginia, near the Appalachian or Allegheny Mountains, on the 10th of May.[3] The rest of his army had arrived on the 17th, after a twenty-seven day march through the woods over a cleared road twelve feet wide.

Up to this time Canada and New England had taken up arms only to dispute the territory where trade with the savages was carried on, and that without even a declaration of war. But what was unknown in Canada was well known in New England, where, as we have mentioned before, the arrival of Braddock in New England was with hostile intent, and followed out a program that the cabinet of London had long planned-since the year 1752, when France and England, respectively, had a discussion of rights in the cabinet. The credulous belief of France in the deceptive replies of England, which entrusted its ambassador Lord Albemarle with the mission of maintaining its present

---

of the colonial troops and regular army. The regular officers had a difficult time supporting the lifestyle to which they were accustomed due to the high prices in Canada. They saw the colonial officers as not only having the advantage of business interests in the colony, but also some were involved in the corruption that caused the economic problems. In addition, the gentlemen of France would not elevate their rustic cousins to their social level.

[3]Braddock reached Fort Cumberland, May 10, 1755 (PHC).

state of good will of the court of France, was
the reason the French did not escape the mis-
fortunes which followed.

It was also mentioned before, that the
English had begun hostilities in the territory
of Acadia in 1750, and that in the same year
traders had settled in French territory in
Upper Canada. In 1751, the Governor General
was obliged to have four traders arrested there
and sent as prisoners to France. It was probably these unimportant disputes which caused
the courts of France and England to have a
four-year discussion of property rights. But
the behavior of the court of London during this
period showed complete proof of bad faith. In
1752, they sent secret orders to New England to
attack the French possessions in Canada. The
pretext was to protect the traders and the savages.

The invasion of part of their lands caused
the French (who learned in 1753 that the Anglo-
Americans were arming) to make reprisals, especially after the new and repeated orders of
1754 from the cabinet in London. It was apparent that Canada must at least put herself on
the defensive to preserve her territory and to
keep open her trade with the savage tribes. We
have likewise seen that England seized Acadia
in the middle of the same year, 1754, and
started their first hostilities at sea. All of
this was without any declaration of war-which
did not come until two years after the debates
in the cabinet. Such was England's treatment
of France. This was not the first time the
English had used illegitimate methods, according to the general opinion held by the other
powers of Europe.

At the time of the declaration of war in
Europe between France and England, various savage tribes of the north, who had been invited
during the previous year to take up the
hatchet, arrived at Fort Duquesne. These savages numbered five hundred. A council was held
when they arrived, in which these savages made
evident their desire to fight for their French
brothers. Tobacco, rifles, powder, and shot

were given them. The second day they divided
into five bands and set out for the settlements
in Virginia, Pennsylvania, and Carolina.
Before leaving, they held their usual war
feast[4] and sang their war song, as described
before. When the meat was cooked, the man in
charge cut it in small bits and distributed a
piece to each warrior. They sat in a circle on
the ground and ate it, as though wishing to do
the same with their common enemy. As there
were several French spectators, including
myself, at this feast, a piece of flesh was
given to each of us, and we had to bite into
it. I did what the others did, and immediately
let the rest of my share fall into the frill of
my shirt without anyone seeing. This is
because the savages would despise any who did
not do as they did on such an occasion, and
would consider them cowards.

After this feast, the savages danced part
of the evening and left the next morning. Ten
Frenchmen were sent with them to know what they
were doing. One of the five parties of savages
came back twelve days later, with only five
scalps and one prisoner. They had lost a man
on the raid, which vexed them very much. After
a few day's rest, they decided to make another
foray against the enemy, to avenge their comrade's death. But they were no luckier on the
second expedition, in which they only got four
scalps. The four other parties also returned,
one after another, with scalps and prisoners,
who received the bastonnade as usual.

It is not astonishing when a strong or
weak band of savages return from war without
success. They are accustomed to consulting

---

[4]For this feast they have a dog or a
prisoner boiled. Upon this occasion it was a
prisoner, who had been bought by promising to
give another in return. It must be noted that
the savages give these feasts only when they
are at a great assembly or in large parties
(JCB).

their wizards,[5] household gods, or manitous,[6] before going to war. If they do not get a favorable omen they either do not go, or if they do go, they come back without doing anything. They may return because they have received some slight setback. They do not go back to war before consulting their gods again, to find out if the latter are more favorable in their prognostication. This is always done through the medium of wizards or sorcerers.

At the end of June, word was received that Braddock's army had marched across the Appalachians and was advancing on Fort Duquesne.[7] At the same time more savages came to the fort from the north. They were sent out in small detachments to reconnoiter and keep us informed of the enemy's daily march.

The evening of July 8th, the scouts announced that, in less than two days, the enemy would be in sight of Fort Duquesne. The next day they would ford the Mal Engueulee River[8] four leagues above the fort. At this news, a council was held concerning the course to be followed. It was decided not to wait for the enemy; but to go to meet him in full force, leaving only one hundred soldiers and some savages to guard the fort.

The morning of July 9th the march was begun, eleven hundred strong. Of this number, three hundred and fifty were French men, and seven hundred and fifty were savages. The whole force was commanded by Captains Beaujeu,[9]

---

[5]These are usually old men who practice sorcery. More will be told of them at the end of these travels, when their homes and habitations will receive mention (JCB).

[6]The savage gods and divinities will be explained at the end of these travels (JCB).

[7]Braddock's expedition was in 1755, not in 1756 (HRC).

[8]The Monongahela River (PHC).

[9]Daniel Hyacinthe Lienard de Beaujeu, 1711-1754, had come to Fort Duquesne to relieve

Dumas,[10] Lemercier, and others. Commander
Contrecoeur remained in the fort with the garrison of a hundred soldiers and as many savages. The army marched through the woods in
three columns to meet the enemy, with our
scouts always in the advance. At noon, the
army halted when the news came that part of the
enemy's army, with its artillery had crossed
the river, and had halted to await the rear
guard and the baggage train. We were then only
a quarter league from them. Immediately the
order was given to advance in double-quick
time, and to attack the enemy simultaneously
from the front and both flanks. This order was
hastily carried out. The savages shouted their
war cry, and the French opened fire with a volley, which was followed by a volley from the
savages. The enemy, taken by surprise, formed
a line of battle, and fired their artillery.
De Beaujeu was killed by the first volley; and
the savages, terrified by the unfamiliar noise
of the cannon, took flight momentarily. But
Captain Dumas took command immediately after
Sieur de Beaujeu's death, and encouraged the
French. The savages saw the steadfastness of
the Frenchmen and no longer heard the cannon,
which the French had seized. They, therefore,
returned to charge the enemy, following the
French example, and forced them to retreat
after two hours of fierce combat, leaving two
thousand men dead on the battlefield. The

Contrecoeur.

[10]Jean Daniel Dumas was born in Agenais,
France c. 1712. He had been a captain in the
Agenais Regiment but came to Canada in 1750 as
a marine captain. After the death of Beaujeu,
he replaced Contrecoeur as governor of the Ohio
region. In 1757, he organized marine companies
into a battalion, and militia into a brigade
structure, for Montcalm before his attack on
Fort William Henry. He was a brigade commander
at the end of the war. He returned to France
and rose to the rank of field marshal in 1780.

English hastily crossed the river, where many
were killed by the never-ending hail of bullets
upon them.

In his flight, the enemy lost artillery,
baggage train, and fifteen flags, as well as
the military chest. The cannons, nine in number, were spiked on the battlefield as soon as
they were captured. General Braddock was
wounded in the battle, and taken away by the
fugitives in a coach, which was with the rear
guard on the other side of the river. It was
indeed a fancy article, absolutely useless in
the forest and mountains where it was the first
one ever to be seen.

After the defeat of the enemy, which was
not thought worth following up, the sixteen
baggage wagons, laden with munitions, food, and
rum, were pillaged. Some of the savages became
intoxicated, and the French had to smash the
barrels to avoid disorder which would inevitably have happened without this wise precaution.
The Indians were the first to discover the
military chest. They did not know the value of
money, and scattered it right and left in the
forest. The French began to gather it up and
to search the dead. Among the dead were one
hundred and five officers, whose belongings
were most in demand.

The night was passed, guarding the battlefield in profound silence, because we did not
know if the enemy would reappear. The men were
seated, two at the foot of each tree. Near the
tree, where a comrade and I were seated, was a
man who began to yawn and talk in the savage
tongue, cursing the English. At first, when he
yawned, we thought he was a wounded Englishman;
but when he spoke, we knew he was a savage who
had fallen into a drunken sleep. We feared,
however, that if he heard us move, he would
suppose we were enemies, and with that notion
rush at us with blows of his tomahawk. We
decided to remain on the defensive.

Shortly after, as the man went on talking,
we said to him very quietly, "Comrade, we are
your French brothers, and have fought the
English with you. All your brothers are here

watching the battlefield until daybreak. You
seem to have had good rum, which has made you
ill and put you to sleep. Like us, you are
here among the dead. For your own sake make no
noise. You may be mistaken for an enemy and
killed."

The savage, who was Shawnee, replied "Qui
hela" (which means, that is true); "but I want
to go away, not stay among these dead dogs."

We urged him to wait for daylight, and he
decided to stay with us. When dawn appeared,
they beat the long roll of drums, and the whole
force was up and about. The savage whom we had
talked to during the night gave us his hand as
a sign of friendship, and went to join the members of his tribe nearby. The French assembled, and when there was no sign of the enemy,
took the road back to Fort Duquesne with the
spoils of the foe.

In this battle the French lost eleven men
and had twenty-two wounded. The savages lost
two men and had twenty wounded. They took sixteen prisoners. They were forbidden to scalp
the dead, who were buried with care. When the
battle was over, three hundred of the savages
returned to their villages, taking along the
sixteen prisoners. The rest of the savages
remained to make raids on English settlements.

General Braddock made the same mistake as
Baron Dieskau by arranging his troops in formal
battle order in the middle of the forest. In
this way they could not make an effective
attack, and ran the risk of being overcome, as
did happen. This was the opinion of the French
Canadians, from which it may be concluded that
it is wiser to use the fighting methods of the
country you are in.

If General Braddock failed in his enterprise, it was not the same with the army
entrusted to Shirley. It had succeeded in taking Fort Niagara on the 26th of June previous,
after an eleven day siege. Two hundred men in
garrison there were commanded by Sieur Pouchot,
captain in the regiment of Bearn. The French
were allowed to depart with the honors of war.

Shirley guarded this post until further orders, which were not long in coming."

We learned during the month of August that a French army of two thousand men commanded by Monsieur Bourlamarque, had appeared early in the month before Chouaguin, and English fort located on the shores of Lake Ontario, twenty-five leagues below Niagara.[12] The French army blockaded and besieged the fort by land. At the end of a week, Fort Oswego-as the English call it-capitulated, and the garrison left, promising not to serve against the French during the war. Eighty cannons were found in this fort. It seemed to be a warehouse, for not half of the cannons were mounted or even used during the siege. The fort was destroyed immediately, and the French retired. They lost forty men in the siege, and General Bourlamarque was wounded in the shoulder. The enemy lost six hundred men and twelve hundred capitulated, so that the garrison had contained altogether eighteen hundred men.

This victory made Sieur Shirley abandon Fort Niagara at once, and the French regained possession of it with a detachment of one hundred men.

During September several bands of savages were sent out from Fort Duquesne to raid English settlements. They took some prisoners and scalps, and burned several settlements.

The English for their part also sent out bands of Iroquois savages toward Fort Duquesne. One of these bands watched us so closely that they succeeded in taking three scalps from men cutting wood about five arpents from the fort.

So passed the remainder of the campaign. Things were very quiet all during the winter, a

---

"Shirley did not capture Fort Niagara, but abandoned his expedition against it, after a council at Oswego on September 27, 1755 (PHC).

[12]Montcalm attacked and captured Fort Oswego in August, 1756 (PHC).

season when the English made no attempt upon any post in Canada.

XI

*Without some unique event to establish the
date, it is assumed that this is 1757. Aside
from the coming and going of raiding parties,
life at Fort Duquesne must have been normal for
a frontier post. Captain Dumas left this fort
to serve with the main army whose objective was
Fort William Henry, which was captured in
August. Dumas was replaced by Francois
Marchand, Sieur de Ligneris. He was the last
commandant of Fort Duquesne and French Ohio.*

In March, a convoy arrived at Fort
Duquesne, with food and one hundred and eighty
men as reinforcements. At the same time, the
order was received to use economy; considering
the difficulty of transportation, which might
become impractical if Fort Niagara were recap-
tured by the English, who abandoned it only
through fear the year before.

At this time, I was made storekeeper of
the trade goods. This job was very advantageous for me, as I was in the position to do
favors. This suited my disposition well
enough. I had various opportunities for doing
favors for the young officers, among others.

I also did favors for some of the savages,
who showed their gratitude by bringing me game.
They took care to supply me with all I wanted.
As a result, I could give part of it to a few
Frenchmen, which was a source of satisfaction
to me.

It is unfortunate, as I have said before,
that there is no gratitude in the hearts of
people you favor. Here is another example.

Two Shawnee savages, who were my trustees
and, as such, were given all they needed, one
day suggested a hunting trip to me. As my job
required constant attention, I could not leave
without the commander's permission. I therefore had to ask for it. I got permission with-

out difficulty; but for one day only, with the
request that I return early. Accordingly, I
got ready to leave next morning and gave my two
guides tobacco, powder, lead, and some bread
for the day's journey. The three of us finally
started on our way at eight o'clock in the
morning. When we had gone three leagues into
the woods, they pointed out a trail to the west
for me to follow. One savage went to the east,
and the other went to the south, promising to
meet me two hours later.

I was alone for scarcely an hour, when I
saw four savages coming toward me. They told
me I was their prisoner and should follow them.
I had to do it, but not without inward qualms
about what might be in store for me. But the
thought occurred that my two men might have
played me a scurvy trick with the idea of getting a few dollars from me.

My surmise was later verified, though not
the same day. The four savages who had captured me made me walk until nightfall, when
they stopped to camp. They built a fire and
invited me to eat. I recognized by their language that they were of the same tribe as my
two men. This reassured me, because I understood their speech. I decided to ask if they
did not recall that I had given them provisions
at Fort Duquesne. They smiled at my question
and did not answer. I immediately felt that my
suspicions were well-founded but I was only
half convinced, for I had to spend the night
with them. When they asked me why I would not
eat, I answered, "When the soul is sick, what
is the use of eating!" My answer drew a reply
that I should not be uneasy, and that no harm
would happen to me. Then, not wanting to eat,
I tried to sleep; but did not sleep well, for I
was worried and agitated. In this way, I
passed the night.

Early next morning, I was surprised to see
my two men arrive. They tried to convince me
that they had been looking for me ever since
they had left, and had not dared to return
without me. As I was absolutely convinced they
had betrayed me purposely, I told them that

they knew well what had happened, and that they had used this scheme to get presents from me. Immediately after my answer, they conferred privately with my captors, and told me I could be free for a trifle. If I would promise to give it, on my word of honor, the four would gladly take me back. I agreed if they would take me back to the fort. I must, however, tell Ononthio (the commander) all about it because he loved the truth, and one must not lie to him or he would be very angry. At this, we all set out to the fort and reached there at three in the afternoon.

When he saw us, the commander expressed surprise that I had not returned the night before. I told him the reason. He reproached the savages and forbade me to give them anything. My sentiments were the same; but knowing how vindictive the savages are when you break your word to them, I decided to keep my promise, at least in part. My two men got only a bit of tobacco, while I gave the four others each a shirt and some tobacco. I told the two who had betrayed me that they should quit bringing me game. I no longer wanted it. They came back, however, bringing some. I would not accept it, for I had taken on two other savages of the Loup tribe who did the same work, to the great regret of the first two. They did what they could to be friendly again, but I was unrelenting.

The savages nearest the Ohio or Belle River, in the north, are five Iroquois tribes already mentioned. Near Fort Duquesne are the Shawnees and the Loups. Going down the river toward New Orleans are the Illinois, the Missouries, the Alabamas, the Mingoes, the Arkancas, the Osages, the Natchitoches, and the Natchez. The Natchez are a cruel tribe, who once did as much harm as they could to the French, and massacred them in their settlements in 1730. They would undoubtedly all have been destroyed in one night, had not a woman of the tribe warned the Frenchman whom she loved. He told the commander about it, who immediately called all his men to arms. He had cannon

aimed and fired on the savages when they
approached. They were forced to give up the
plan, when they realized that the French were
on their guard and not asleep. The other savage tribes near Louisiana are the Cenis, the
Choctaws, the Chickasaws, the Cherokee, the
Natchigamis, the Tonikas, the Sioux, the
Yazoos, and others.

As many as seven or eight hundred members
of these tribes assembled and came to Fort
Duquesne in June to go to war against the
English. Their unexpected arrival made us so
distrustful that we held council with them
under the cannons of the fort, although these
tribes manifested much good will. For six
weeks they continued to make raids on the
English settlements, where they took many prisoners and scalps. They gave nineteen prisoners
to the commander.

When they wanted to go home, another council was held to ask them to come back. They
refused, because it was too far and such a long
trip was very fatiguing. Besides, they had to
cultivate their fields to support themselves
and their families. I was at this council,
where I acted as secretary. I wrote down the
speeches and the replies on both sides, according to each belt or string of wampum signified,
backed up by each rather concise speech concerning their wish to maintain peace and
friendship with the French. At the end of this
council, each man was given a shirt, tobacco,
and a small glass of brandy. The interpreter
explained, for the commander, that he had no
more, that he had been saving this for a long
time. These final words made them utter sighs
of disappointment and regret, saying that it
was a great pity. So ended this council, with
which they were well satisfied. The next day
they left with their prisoners and scalps.

In general, all the savages liked brandy.
They have a very strong desire for this liquor,
and it is a deadly present for them, because
they become raging mad as soon as they have
drunk it. They fight and kill each other.
Consequently, the smallest amount possible is

given them, for fear of destroying their character, as they express it.

The following is an example of this liquor's effect on the savages. The indiscretion of some Frenchmen was the cause.

A Frenchman, who had a pint of liquor at his disposal, gave a small glass full to a savage he was entertaining, without being careful to hide his bottle. A moment later the savage asked for a little more. The Frenchman hesitated, but finally gave it to him. As a result, the savage became drunk and insisted on having still more. The Frenchman refused him absolutely. When the Indian started hunting the bottle, the Frenchman objected. A quarrel began between them, which ended in the savage threatening him with a knife. The Frenchman, angered by this threat, tried to eject the man who had been abusing him.

Without provocation, the savage quickly drew his knife and wounded the Frenchman in the arm. He would probably have continued his attack, had not several Frenchmen come to the rescue at that moment. They seized the savage, quickly disarmed him, and took him to the commander. The savage told the latter that the Frenchman had made him drink and then refused him any more, although he still had some. The commander sent for the Frenchman and reprimanded him severely, forbidding him to give savages anything to drink. To show the savage that the Frenchman had no more brandy to give him, he resorted to a trick. For this, he put water in a bottle, brought it out for the savage to see, and said, "Here is the bottle of liquor which did you harm. It will never do it again." At the same time he walked to the doorstep and poured out the water from the bottle. The savage was greatly vexed at seeing his hopes frustrated by this trick. The Frenchman was likewise punished by being imprisoned until the next day.

Because of this trifling affair, the garrison was forbidden to give any brandy to the savages under penalty of confiscation and a month's imprisonment. It was well known that

several Frenchman had received some in the convoy. It could not be taken from them without
injustice. The more sensible kept a small supply, but the more self-seeking exchanged it for
game which the savages brought them. It was
this trading that occasioned disputes, one of
which very nearly proved fatal to me, although
I was not concerned in it.

Some Frenchmen had given savages brandy to
drink, either as an act of friendship or for a
selfish motive. One of the savages was told,
merely to get rid of him, that there was no
more; but if he wanted liquor he would have to
go to the storekeeper, who had a supply.

This savage, already partly drunk, came to
find me. His first words were: "My brother, I
want a drink very much. Give me a sip of
brandy. I know that you have some, because a
Frenchman told me so. Do me a favor and give
me some."

I told him there was none at my disposal.
He would have to ask Ononthio (the commander).
Dissatisfied with my answer, the man finally
tried to find it for himself. I stopped him
for which I had sufficient reason that it would
be dangerous to let the savages know of the
stores I guarded.

Like a madman, he drew his tomahawk from
his belt and tried to strike me on the head. I
backed away, raising my arm to parry the blow,
and was slightly wounded in the left wrist.
This so aroused my anger that I picked up a
stick near at hand, and gave the rascal a hard
rap on the head. He fell down, but, lest he
get up and attack me again, I gave him a second
blow. This made him unconscious, so that I
thought him dead.

Becoming worried, I quickly closed the
door of the room where this affair happened. I
was afraid other savages might find out about
it, in which case I would risk being killed by
them. The only witness to the incident having
been my clerk, we together decided to carry the
lifeless body out the back door, and lay it on
some timbers. We did this without anyone

seeing us, and kept the whole affair a complete
secret.

The wretch was, however, not as dead as we
thought. He was discovered an hour or so later
by some savages of his tribe. They saw that he
was unconscious, and carried him away. I saw
them take him, and began to fear he would
remember me. He sobered up during the night
and complained about his head. He remembered
drinking brandy, but not who had given it to
him. He could given no answer to the various
questions of his comrades, because he could not
remember. They came to the conclusion, which
convinced him, that he had injured himself on
the timbers where he was found. I saw him
walking with his head bandaged up, and avoided
meeting him. But when I realized that he did
not recall anything, I felt much relieved.

Another Frenchman who likewise manhandled
a savage some days later, in connection with a
similar refusal to give brandy, was not so
lucky. For the man he mistreated recognized
him, and sought an opportunity to take revenge.
Since there was reason to fear that this savage
would go to the extreme in his revenge, the
commander, who had been informed of the facts,
sent the Frenchman secretly to Fort Presque
Isle to get him away from his implacable foe.

For some time there had been an ordinance
in Canada, which prohibited all Frenchmen from
giving brandy to the savages in trade, or otherwise, under penalty of confiscation of the
liquor and exemplary punishment. The same pen-
alties were enforced for mistreatment of the
savages. Although this ordinance was renewed
each time there was a new governor general of
the country, that did not stop the trade in
brandy, for it was carried on in upper Canada
far from the cities. The voyageurs were, moreover, never prevented from having a supply of
it for their own needs; for this liquor, which
keeps up their courage, helps them to get
favors, particularly when they have nothing
else to give the savages in return for the
game. If brandy is given them, the savages
must not be angered or mistreated, and above

all, not killed, whatever the misdeed. I cite
here a severe punishment meted out some time
ago in Montreal, because of such an offense. I
did not witness the incident, but several people told me about it, and assured me it was
true.

A Frenchman killed a savage in a quarrel.
Some members of his tribe carried a complaint
about it to the governor of the town. Either
from policy, or for some other reason, he asked
the accusers if they could identify the mur-
derer. They replied that they could. The governor said, "In that case, bring him to me. In
your presence I shall punish him for his
crime."

The next morning the savages did not fail
to indict the man as the slayer, before the
governor. The official questioned the accused
Frenchman, and asked him if he were guilty of
the murder. Admitting the deed, the slayer
said he had done it in self defense. After
hearing the confession, the governor with no
further formalities had him hung. This drastic
punishment satisfied the savages; but nevertheless it made the French grumble against the
unlawful judgment of the governor. In this
country it has always been thought a bad policy
to punish a Frenchman who uses violence against
the savages, whereas savages can mistreat and
even kill a Frenchman with impunity, incurring
no more than a reprimand.

To tell the truth, the savages are not
encouraged in such actions. Among the English,
it is entirely different. A savage killing an
Englishman, if caught, is punished with death,
while an Englishman is never punished for killing a savage. Perhaps for this reason, more
savage tribes are allied with the French than
the English. But, for their own interests,
savages prefer trading with the English,
because the latter sell their goods at lower
prices.

In June, I was made temporary keeper of
the provision stores. This position enabled me
to augment my income without incurring any
risk.

XII

I have already spoken about the situation of Fort Duquesne. I am now going to tell about its climate and soil; and about the soil along the Ohio.

The climate is mild and temperate, only the month of January being cold. The rains in the spring and fall, however, cause floods, which come from the mountains and fill the Ohio River to a point where it overflows its banks.

The soil is easily cultivated, though I have never seen anything grown there except maize or Indian corn, peas, beans, pumpkins, and tobacco as good as that grown in Virginia. South of the Ohio are wide prairies, called the Scioto, where there are quicksands in some areas. Game and fish are abundant a little further down. The game consists of deer, elk, bear, buffalo, red-legged partridges, squirrels, and various species of ducks, particularly flying ducks (?). Many crocodiles or caymans' are found along the banks of the Ohio and Mississippi.

To the east of Fort Duquesne are the Appalachian or Allegheny mountains, about which we have already spoken. New England is beyond them. In the Ohio and its tributaries, they usually fish for carp, eels, pike, sturgeon, and brill.

All the varieties of trees are very beautiful in the Ohio country. Here there are two species of pine, the white pine and the red; four kinds of firs, bearing the names of silver

---

'This amphibious animal is very voracious and dangerous, especially in the water. It has very hard scales; and to kill it, you must strike it in the shoulder joint or in the eyes (JCB).

spruce, red spruce, the pereuse and the French
fir; two kinds of cedar, white and red; two
kinds of oak, white and red; maple trees, male
and female; wild cherry trees ash trees, plane-
trees, hornbeams, beeches, three kinds of walnut trees, two kinds of elms, plum trees, and
other vegetation. Almost all of these are also
grown in Canada.

The maple is the most remarkable of all
these trees, because every year, in February
and March, there exudes from this tree an abundant flow of a delicious, sweet and clear liquid which is fragrant and very wholesome. The
tree will die, however, if it is used too
often. The method for extracting the juice
from it is quite simple. When the sap in the
trees begins to rise to any extent, a slanting
groove is cut about three feet from the ground,
and a knife blade, or piece of wood shaped like
a blade of a knife, is inserted. The juice
runs down this spout so abundantly that twenty-
five pails of it may be drawn from a healthy
tree between sunrise and sunset. The liquid
flows into a large vessel to be emptied into a
large kettle as it fills. These are placed
over a hot fire to boil the juice which becomes
first a syrup, then moist sugar. This amounts
to twelve or fifteen pounds a day, and while
moist is put into wooden bowls to harden into a
round loaf.

Maple sap can be drawn from the same tree
for five or six consecutive days, if care is
taken to make new grooves every day always on
the side toward the noonday sun. This must be,
too, when it has been cold the night before,
and when there is bright sunshine without a
cold, fierce wind. It can be determined that
the tree contains no more sap when the sap
appears whitish and runs slowly.

When it is at that stage, vinegar or a
drink like cider can be made from it, if you go
on extracting, but it still must be boiled down
into sugar.

Maple sap must be cooked for two full
hours to make syrup, and two more hours to make
sugar, which is always brown. It is very good

for the lungs and never causes heartburn.
Maple sugar is made into small cakes like
chocolate so that it can more easily be carried
on trips. It keeps a long time if dry, otherwise becomes moldy, spoiling because of dampness. Maple trees usually have large growths
on them, which are cut and dried in the sun,
making a sort of touchwood which the Canadians
call tondre.[2]

The plane-tree, the wild cherry, the ash,
and the walnut, also produce sap that yields
sugar but as the flow is much less and the
sugar not so good, it is almost never made.
Maple sugar, therefore, is most used in Canada,
as much as white sugar is used. This comes
from San Domingo.[3] Maple sugar is easily
digested.

I have told about hunting turkeys, bears,
beavers, and squirrels, and more will be
related about some other game. But I shall now
tell about hunting buffalo.

This sport is very enjoyable. The buffalo
ordinarily herd together on the prairies, occasionally as many as two to three hundred. When
this hunting is to be engaged in, several hunters join up and stretch nets made of whitewood
bark or birch bark. These are fastened to
stakes driven in the ground to form a barrier.
After the nets are stretched, the hunters beat
the woods, either on foot or on horseback, over
a large area, in order to drive buffalo into
the nets. As the animals begin to flee, they

---

[2]Tinder (PHC).

[3]Everyone knows that sugar came originally
from India, from whence it was taken to Arabia
in the thirteenth century. From there it was
brought to Egypt, Cyprus, Sicily, Provence,
Spain, and finally to San Domingo by Americus
Vespucius in 1497 or 1498. Chocolate
originated in Mexico, and was brought to France
by the Spanish in 1520. Coffee originated in
India. The first known in France arrived at
Marseilles in 1644 (JCB).

are followed, an inevitably stopped in their
course and thrown by the nets. Some of the
hunters, who have been lying in wait, quickly
rush to hamstring them with tomahawk blows,
thus mastering them. They bleed them immediately.

At mating time, the animals attack hunters, who skillfully escape by taking refuge
behind trees. The buffalo, with its head lowered, rushes furiously and cracks its horns
against the tree it was headed for. The
hunter, waiting with tomahawk in hand, at once
aims several blows at its head between the two
horns, in order to fell the animal to the
ground. As soon as it is down, the buffalo's
throat is cut.

It must not be thought that a great number
of buffalo are taken in the nets; for the nets
very often are broken by their strength. When
they have made an opening, they dash through it
and escape. It is, however, a fact that some
are always caught. They are also hunted one at
a time, and this individual hunting is more
difficult, because the animal has a very keen
sense of smell. The hunter must go down wind
to get near. It is very timid; though it
becomes enraged when it is wounded, or when the
cows have newborn calves.

The buffalo has short black horns, and
long hair under its muzzle and on its head,
covering its eyes and giving it a hideous
appearance. On its back there is a hump, which
starts at the haunches and grows larger toward
the shoulders. The hump is covered with long
reddish hair. The rest of the body is covered
with curly black wool. The animal is very
broad across the chest and narrow at the rump,
with a short tail and neck, and a large head.
The meat of the cow is more tender and better
eating that that of the bull.

There are in the neighborhood of the Ohio
many humming birds scarcely as large as olives.
There are also glow-worms or fireflies, as well
as swarms of bees in the trees with their
honey. The savages of these parts call bees

English flies. These are more common in Carolina, which is also true of silkworms.

Here various species of snakes may be seen, particularly in marshy places. Grasshoppers cover the earth during almost six months of the year. Mosquitos are the most troublesome insects. They are called stingers and gnats in Europe. To keep them off, it is necessary to rub lard on the face, hands, and body; the insect sticks to the grease and dies instantly. Another way to keep them off, particularly after a rain when they are the most numerous, is by a heavy smudge, but this method does not kill them.

There are many wild grapevines, which climb to the tree tops. The size, color, and quality of the grapes depends on the situation of the ground. They have a rather wild taste; but wine could be made of them, if the vines were cultivated. I tried it and succeeded in making forty pints. The wine is not found bad after it has worked about three days. It retains a tart flavor; is without much body; and doesn't have a bad taste. It neither improves nor loses its sharp flavor when it has stood for two months.

Among the medicinal plants growing in the Ohio territory, the fleawort[4] is worthy of note. Travelers anywhere in Canada must be able to recognize it not because of its good qualities, but rather to avoid it. The effects of this plant are more or less apparent on the susceptibility of those who touch it. Some it does not affect at all, while others develop a slow fever, lasting about two weeks, and accompanied by a very uncomfortable itching, with scabs over the whole body. The parts affected finally appears leprous, and swells so much that the hands cannot be used during the two weeks the malady spreads. No other remedy than patience is known for it. The fleawort, which

[4]Poison ivy (PHC).

has no other name in Canada, is somewhat similar to the hemlock.

Another plant, ginseng, is well known there. Its root is very good for colds and for stomach disorders, when steeped in bouillon or white wine. It also stimulates perspiration, and is sometimes used as a condiment or spice in stews. The maidenhair fern is also commonly found throughout the country.

Very good tobacco[5] comes from the country around the Ohio; especially in Virginia, Carolina, and Maryland, where the soil is adapted to it, giving it superior quality. In this region it is most often raised, and tobacco from here has the highest reputation in Canada. The Illinois (and particularly the Natchez) also grow very fine tobacco, equal in strength and quality to the Virginian tobacco. The latter is yellowish, while that grown by the Illinois and Natchez is very black and rich, and of very good aroma.

This is the way tobacco is cultivated, especially in Virginia. First, in March, the seed is scattered in hotbeds in clusters. When it has grown four or five inches high, it is transplanted to a suitable field where the earth has been prepared and worked into mounds. In each mound a tobacco seedling is planted, always spaced three or four feet apart on all sides. Care must be taken to remove all the bad leaves and all the leaves which might interfere with its growth, beginning with the bottom leaves because of the dampness of the soil. The stalk is broken or cut to keep it from growing too high. The shoots are cut as fast as they grow, and only eight or ten leaves

---

[5]Originating in Mexico, it was discovered by the Spanish in 1520, taken to Africa, Asia, Europe and several parts of America. First brought to France by Francois Nicot, French ambassador to Portugal in 1560, the seed was given by him to Catherine De Medicis, Henry II's widow, who successfully planted it (JCB).

are left to mature in August, at the time the
stalk is cut at the foot, and left on the
ground to dry in the sun a few days. After
this, the stalks are carried to barns where
they are hung up to dry and ripen. Then they
pick off the ripest leaves, and pile them up in
small packets. The finest leaves are selected
and put together, and called first quality.
The inferior leaves are kept separate. The
packets, tied by the stems and placed in a
press, are finally packed in casks or barrels.
In this way, there are three grades of tobacco
produced in Virginia.

Some growers remove the center stem from
the leaves and moisten the leaves slightly with
salt water, or an infusion made from an herb
whose leaves resemble tea leaves. The choice
leaves are made into rolls such as we see in
France. Tobacco will mildew if it is permitted
to become too wet when it is being prepared. A
row of four stalks with nine leaves on each is
enough to make a pound of tobacco. When it is
desired to save seeds to sow the next year,
fifty to sixty plants are allowed to reach
their full height without breaking off the
tops.

Tobacco culture requires much care.
Mishaps must be guarded against. Care must be
taken to remove the worms that get on tobacco
plants; and to prevent dampness which overheats
it, the strong winds which break the stalks,
and the caterpillars which eat the leaves.
This crop, therefore needs constant attention.

In the autumn of the same year (1757),
there was such a flood on the Ohio River, that
it caused a considerable inundation in the
neighborhood of Fort Duquesne. The water rose
twenty-five feet above usual level, so that it
was five feet deep above the bank, or grounds,
where Fort Duquesne was built.

The flood did not reach the fort, because
at the time it was laid out they foresaw what
might happen and raised the ground it was built
on. The moat around it was, however flooded
with water. This inundation lasted for twelve

hours, starting at noon and steadily rising
until midnight.

Above the fort, on the opposite bank of
the Ohio, a small village had grown up. It
included some sixty wooden cabins where part of
the garrison lodged. I, too, had built a little cottage there, in which I sometimes slept;
although I lived at the fort because of my com-
mercial relations with my partner. Curiosity
led me to spend the night of the flood there,
to get a better impression of it. Everyone
had, however, taken care to empty his cabin.
Mine contained only a bed, a table, and two
chairs. I made a good fire there. About
eleven o'clock in the evening I became sleepy
and threw myself on the bed fully dressed. I
put a lamp on a chair beside me, and a ladder
upon which I could climb, in case of necessity,
to the loft which was over the ground floor. I
finally fell so sound asleep that that first my
fire, and then my lamp, were extinguished by
the water. It would soon have reached my bed,
had not a loud noise outside wakened me. Since
neither the fire nor the lamp were to be seen.
I reached down toward the ground and felt the
water. I quickly climbed to the loft, and
looked through the window. I saw many persons
in bateaux on the flats with torches, taking
people to higher ground. Then I called out,
and a man with a boat came and took me to land
like the others. Already several cabins had
been swept away by the raging waters and I was
afraid of losing mine, which was no stronger
than the rest. It was, however, left standing
unharmed.

Like the others, I was astonished to see
the water recede as rapidly as it had risen;
for at eight o'clock in the morning it was no
longer overflowing the banks. Now everyone
could go back on foot to his cabin, except the
men who had none left. It was discovered that
fifteen cabins had been swept away by the
water, but that was soon remedied by building
new cabins, a task which was finished in two or
three days. Nevertheless, the water in the
river took several days to recede. This was

the only flood of any consequence I saw during
my stay at Fort Duquesne.

The rest of this campaign went by quietly
at the fort.   Bands of savages were constantly
sent out to raid the English settlements.   It
was learned that Governor Vaudreuil, together
with General Montcalm and other high-ranking
officers, was laying out offensive and defensive plans to meet the English plans for the
ensuing campaign of which we had been informed.

XIII

J.C.B. places the French attack on Fort William Henry in this year which is, of course, incorrect. It happened in 1757. Also in error is the defeat of Aubry near Presque Isle. This is probably a reference to the battle at La Belle Famille, near Fort Niagara in 1759. His reports of Aubry's fight against Grant, the expedition against Louisbourg, and the attack on Fort Carillon (Ticonderoga) are correct as to the year, although there are errors in the details. J.C.B. leaves Fort Duquesne before the English, under General Forbes, make their final advance forcing Ligneris, in late November, to destroy the fort and withdraw to the north.

Year 1758: This campaign opened in March, when a convoy of food and munitions with a reinforcement of one hundred and fifty men arrived at Fort Duquesne. The Governor General had learned that the English were planning to drive the French from the Ohio.

Shortly after, five hundred savages came from the region of Michillimakinac. The day after they arrived, we held a council with them, in which they explained their desire to fight against the English. They were made welcome for their goodwill and were given tobacco, powder, and shot, as was customary. They had a war feast, boiling a dog in water, and dividing it among them. Then they danced part of the night.

Next morning, they split up into five bands and set out in various directions to the English settlements. One band returned twenty days later with forty prisoners and one hundred and twenty scalps. This party had laid waste to two settlements in Virginia. Their prisoners were fortunate in escaping the bastonnade,[1] as there were no savages at the fort when they arrived.

The other four parties, one after the other, came in some days later, with many scalps and prisoners. These prisoners were not so lucky as the first, for they had to undergo the bastonnade from the savages who had first arrived. Of all these prisoners, only seven were given to the commander. The savages kept the rest and took them away, as well as the scalps.

It was rather general custom among the savage tribes, not to continue warfare when they have been victorious. This is because they fear their tutelary gods will not be favorable or will punish them. It is also customary, when they have been victorious at war, for the chief of the war party to leave a tomahawk on the battlefield. The emblems of the tribe and the number of warriors he had with him are indicated on its handle. He does this as much to show valor, as to defy his enemies to come and attack him. Some tribes merely make the same signs on a tree, stripping off the outside bark. It is said, however, that this is only done in wars with other savages. It is seldom done when they fight Europeans, unless there are hostile savages fighting along with the Europeans.

The prisoners taken are either adopted, enslaved, or condemned to death. Slaves do most of the menial work, such as cutting firewood, cultivating the fields, harvesting, pounding Indian corn or maize to make sagamite,[2] cooking, mending the hunters' shoes, carrying their game, and, in general, anything that women do. The women are in charge of the slaves, and deny them food if they are lazy. Adoption is undertaken by a family which has lost a man in battle, and wants to replace him

---

[1]Running the gantlet [gauntlet] (PHC).
[2]A sort of hasty pudding (JCB).

by a prisoner who seems suitable to them. The
women are left free to select this prisoner,
especially women who have lost their husbands.
In this case, they choose the prisoner to be
adopted, even from those condemned to be burned
(for there is no other form of execution among
the savages); and in these circumstances, a
woman need only throw her blanket over the condemned man's body. Though he be trussed up and
ready for execution, that is enough to prove
that he has been adopted. The woman unties him
and takes him away without objection from the
executioners.

A messenger from Quebec brought word that
in June an English fleet commanded by Admiral
Boscawen had appeared before Louisbourg, the
principal fort on Isle Royale, with a landing
force of sixteen thousand men commanded by
Generals Wolfe and Amherst.[3] They immediately
began a siege lasting many days, which the
French commander Drucourt withstood with great
valor and courage, despite a heavy cannonade
and bombardment. During this siege, the commanders' wife performed great feats of valor;
firing cannons and holding back several
onslaughts. But in spite of this fine defense,
the place could not hold out and had to capitulate with the honors of war. This garrison
contained twenty-four hundred soldiers and four
thousand inhabitants.

Isle Royale, also called Cape Breton, has
been mentioned before. It is thirty leagues
long and twenty-two leagues across at its widest part. Waves dash at the foot of small
separate rocks with which its entire coast
bristles. All the ports open to the east. On
the southern side, except for the mountainous
parts, the land surface is rather soft. It is
mossy and wet everywhere. The great dampness

---

[3]Admiral Boscawen and General Amherst
landed in Gabarus Bay on June 8, 1758, to begin
the siege of Louisbourg (PHC).

of the soil causes mists, without making the
air unhealthy. The climate is very cold.

Louisbourg, the capital of this island, is
built on an oblong neck of land jutting out
toward the sea. The fortress is three quarters
of a league around, and much of it is built of
French stone. The French came into possession
of it in 1713, and fortified it in 1720. This
island's population, at the time of the capture, was ten thousand inhabitants; six thousand of whom were distributed among Fort
Dauphin, Port Toulouse, Nerika, and other
beaches[4] suitable for drying codfish. The
remaining four thousand people live in
Louisbourg.

The people of this island have never
engaged in agriculture. The soil of the island
is not suitable for it. Only a few soup vege-
tables are planted; but they are of a very good
flavor. The scarcity of pasture keeps the
herds from increasing there. The energy of the
people is taken up with codfishing and mining
the coal produced in this country.

During the month of July, Sieur Aubry,[5]
captain of the Louisiana troops, arrived at
Fort Duquesne with two hundred and forty men,
and several large boats carrying ten tons of
both provisions and merchandise. Four thousand
pounds of Natchez tobacco, which belonged to
the guide, were part of the load. They were
offered to me for six thousand livres. I knew
that the owner would rather sell it wholesale
than retail, and that only I and my partner
were in a position to purchase it. I offered
him half of his price in ready cash. When the
salesman tried to haggle, I said it must be yes
or no and that he could get no more for it, and
turned my back on him. The man decided to let
me have it, and I paid him at once. About an

---

[4]In Canada a "grave" (beach) is more
elevated than an ordinary "greve," and is less
subject to inundation (JCB).

[5]Charles Philippe, Sieur de Aubry.

hour later, a trader, who knew about the purchase I had just made, looked me up to buy the
goods from me. I told him I wanted six thousand francs for it. he took up my offer and
the business was finished in such a way that I
made a profit of a few thousand crowns, without
looking at the goods or running any risk of
loss.

A few days after Captain Aubry's arrival,
an English army of a thousand men, led by
General Grant,[6] came to attempt a surprise
assault on Fort Duquesne. To draw out the garrison, his first move was to have a general
alarm beaten on the Ohio side. Meanwhile, the
greater part of his army waited on the
Monongahela side to assail the fort as soon as
he saw the garrison depart. But his plan was
thwarted.

Captain Aubry led about five hundred men
out from the fort; but instead of marching in
the direction of the beating drums, he advanced
along the Monongahela River, and suddenly met
the enemy. The battle began at once, and so
vigorously, that the enemy took flight after
three hundred men had fallen. Thirty-five
prisoners were taken. The savages gave the

---

[6]This name is given as "Gicent" in the
printed French version, but this is evidently
an error of the transcriber. Grant was a
major, not a general, who was defeated at Fort
Duquesne, September 10, 1758. He had been
reconnoitering rather than attempting a
surprise attack (PHC).

Grant's purpose was to separate the
Indians from the French, even if it took an
attack on their villages in the vicinity of the
fort. General Forbes continued this policy
during his advance later in the year. His
success in drawing the Indians away from the
French allowed him to take the remains of Fort
Duquesne from which the French had retreated
and destroyed.

seven they captured to the commander of the
fort.

The French had but one man killed and five
wounded. The reason for the small loss on the
French side was that they fought behind trees,
while the enemy were in the open. This success, with the others won previously in the
Ohio region, should have discouraged the
English from making further attempts, but they
were not disheartened. Powerful levies of
militia were raised in Virginia, Pennsylvania,
Carolina, and New Jersey. Savages were sent
toward For Duquesne in hope of taking prisoners
among the French engaged in chopping wood
daily.

I was walking one day along the Ohio bank
above Fort Duquesne, and went in the woods to
gather hazelnuts. I had been there only as
short time and was not far away from the
woodchoppers, when I heard two rifle shots and
the whistle of a bullet. I dropped flat on the
ground and did not stir, trying to make out
whether the shots were fired at me or at the
woodchoppers. It was not long before I heard
the deathcry. Then I knew they were not
attacking me, and that a man had been killed
and scalped. This showed the enemy was
retreating. I decided to get back as quick as
possible. No sooner had I left the wood than I
saw several armed Frenchmen running toward me.
When they came up to me, they questioned me,
and I replied that I had seen nothing. I
pointed out the direction the shots came from,
and said a man had certainly been killed, as I
had heard the deathcry. This was soon confirmed, for when they entered the woods, they
found the corpse of a man who had been murdered
and scalped. It was carried to camp, where it
was interred at once; attended, among others,
by the men who had been cutting wood with him
and had escaped to the fort as soon as they had
heard the two rifle shots.

All things were quiet along the Ohio, such
was not the case in the heart of Canada where
we were engaged in fighting the enemy.

During the month of July, a French army of six thousand men commanded by General Montcalm, assisted by Generals Levis and Bourlamarque, advanced to the south of Canada through Lake Champlain as far as Lake Saint Sacrement where the English had built a fort, which they named Fort George; just as they called the lake, Lake George. There, they had twenty-four hundred men in garrison and fifty pieces of artillery. The French army blockaded and besieged it, but this took only a few days. In spite of its resistance, the fort was taken and the garrison released after promising not to serve again during the war.[7] The fort was demolished by the French, who fell back four leagues to Fort Carillon, where they made entrenchments a full rifle shot from the fort, to avoid being surprised by the enemy and to keep them from coming too near the fortifications.

This was a useful and wise precaution which General Montcalm took because he had been warned that the enemy was getting ready to come to Fort Carillon,[8] and he was making preparations to fight them when they arrived.

Not long afterward, the English army, made up of twenty-two thousand men commanded by Generals Loudon and Abercrombie,[9] advanced. The French met them at the edge of the

---

[7]Fort William Henry, at the head of Lake George, was captured by Montcalm in August, 1757. Fort George was built near its site in 1759 (PHC).

[8]Carillon, which the English called Ticonderoga, was located at the end of Lake Champlain. It was a more advanced position than the Fort of Point a la Chevelure, the other French post which was destroyed by the English after the defeat of Baron de Dieskau (JCB). (Crown Point [Fort St. Frederic] was not destroyed then.) (PHC).

[9]Lord Loudon had been recalled before this campaign began. Abercrombie commanded in the Crown Point campaign of 1758 (PHC).

entrenchment which they had prepared. On the
outside there was a strong abattis of very
bushy trees and brush; this was about fifteen
toises thick. The parapet of the entrenchment
was four and a half feet high and eight or nine
feet thick. The French army numbered seven
thousand men. The enemy advanced with fixed
bayonets and tried to break through the abattis
which impeded them. They struggled to accom-
plish this for nearly five hours and then
retreated, leaving four thousand men dead on
the field in the abattis of trees.[10] After
their retreat, the French were satisfied, not
wanting to pursue them. They buried the dead,
and guarded the entrenchments for three days
lest the enemy return to attack. As the latter
did not reappear, the French army withdrew,
leaving at Fort Carillon only two hundred and
fifty men under the command of General
Bourlamargue, who had been wounded in the col-
larbone during the battle. The French lost
very few men, and this engagement brought them
much glory.

During August, various bands of savages
were sent out from Fort Duquesne to raid the
English settlements. They brought back many
prisoners and scalps.

I had been warned in September that I
would shortly be relieved of the position which
I held as storekeeper for merchandise and provisions, and sent back to Quebec. I made the
necessary preparations, beginning with a general inventory of everything in the warehouses
and making up an account of receipts and expen-
ditures. I also settled my accounts with the
trader who was my partner, and told him that,
in view of the fact that I would soon leave
Fort Duquesne and did not know if I should come
back, I had decided to dissolve the partner-
ship. The accounts between us were closed, and

---

[10]Other sources state that nearly 2,000
men were killed in the attack on Ticonderoga,
July 5-6, 1758 (PHC).

as a result I received, both as profit on sales
and as payment for the stock remaining in the
warehouse, the sum of 32,400 francs paid by
drafts on a business representative living in
Montreal. Then I sent the trunk, containing my
effects and ten thousand francs in paper money
of the country, to the storekeeper at Presque
Isle, with the request that he forward it to my
address in Montreal at the first opportunity.

The 21st of October was the date of my
departure from Fort Duquesne, after three
years' residence there. I had earlier made two
profitable trips to this place. I left with a
party of twenty-two men. When I reached
Presque Isle, I took care to find out if my
trunk had been sent on. The storekeeper
replied that he thought that this had been
done; and as I considered this a doubtful
answer, I felt it was necessary to look in the
warehouse. This was filled with various par-
cels that would have required much time to move
and put back in place. I could, therefore,
make only a hasty search. I was convinced that
my trunk had gone on since I did not see it,
and I continued my journey with that assurance.
nevertheless, when we reached Niagara, I
inquired of the storekeeper if he knew anything
about it. He said he had sent on everything he
had received at Presque Isle. Although he did
not mention this particular trunk, I was still
convinced that it had been forwarded to its
destination, and left this post still under
that impression.

The 12th of November, rowing through Lake
Saint Francois, we ran into bitter cold
weather, with such a sharp north wind that we
were frozen fast in the ice. We could not
manoeuver to go forward or backward, and
remained in this predicament for a full hour,
during which nine men had their feet frozen.
The ice became thicker during this interval,
and we decided to risk ourselves upon it with
the aid of our oars and paddles. We were lucky
enough to reach land, which was about two

arpents" away. But this was not without difficulty, for there were weak spots in the ice
which we had to avoid, with the help of the
oars. Fortunately, we were favored by bright
moonlight. The crossing occurred about midnight. We dragged the nine frostbitten men
with no other aid to look for but our courage.
We were not less benumbed with cold when we
reached land and no sooner had we gained the
shore than we cut wood to make a good fire
which warmed us and the frostbitten men during
the night.

When daylight came, we were very much per-
plexed about continuing our journey by land.
We had food enough for a week which would have
been more than enough, had we traveled by
water. But it was not sufficient for the land
journey, since we would have to travel in short
stages on account of our crippled men. We then
decided to send three from our party ahead to a
village of Abenaquis savages, seven leagues
farther down the river, to tell them of our
predicament and ask them to lend us aid. They
did this willingly. Twelve of them came three
days later and brought us game. We ate part of
it, and then made stretchers to carry our
injured men. The Frenchmen and the savages
took turns in carrying them to the village
where we stayed five days. Then the Abenaquis
took us in their canoes and piloted us through
the rapids to Montreal, which we reached on the
24th of that month. The frostbitten men were
immediately taken to the hospital, where they
had to amputate the feet of five men. Two died
after the operation.

When I arrived in this city, my first care
was to hunt for my trunk. It was not to be
found and no one seemed to know anything about
it. I then suspected that it had been delayed
enroute, and wrote to the storekeepers at the
various posts it should have passed through. I
wrote especially to the man at Presque Isle, to

"An arpent is 191.838 English feet.

whom it was first consigned, asking him to make
a thorough search for it, and send it on to me
at once in case it was still in his possession.
I received no answer, although I repeated my
claim for six months. Then I had to resign
myself to this loss which was the first one I
had experienced. I felt it less because I
expected to make it up. Moreover, I had more
important funds (I will tell of them later),
and I had just received the amount of my drafts
which my partner had given me to take to his
business representative.

November 30th, I left Montreal in a party
of ten to go to Quebec. In four days we traveled by water to the town of Three Rivers, and
from there we had to go overland because of the
ice. Despite the extreme cold, our trip was
not too unpleasant because we were cordially
welcomed by the people in the villages through
which we passed. I can truthfully say that
among the Canadians there is universally found
a thoughtful and generous hospitality, which
shelters the traveler from hunger, thirst, and
the cold of winter, and which provides a resting place, all given with such solicitude it
can hardly be refused without offense.

December tenth, we arrived in Quebec. The
next day I went to call on my acquaintances,
who made me very welcome and invited me to several affairs, which I naturally appreciated and
for which I thanked them sincerely.

Some days after my arrival, news came that
Captain Aubry, mentioned before, had encountered the English, while taking two hundred men
from the garrison at Fort Duquesne to Fort de
la Presque Isle.[12] The English came in force

---

[12]This is presumably a distorted account
of the French attempt to raise the English
siege at Fort Niagara in July 1759. A force
under Aubry, de Ligneris, and de Villiers went
from Fort Presque Isle to Niagara, where they
were defeated by the English under Sir William
Johnson. Aubry was wounded, and captured with

against the latter place to force its surrender
and thus keep any help from reaching Fort
Duquesne.   They met the French detachment at
the mouth of the River aux Boeufs, enroute to
reinforce the garrison of Presque Isle.   In a
combat lasting two hours, the French were
defeated.   Captain Aubry and his second in command, Captain Devilliers, were wounded.   The
latter was the brother of Jumonville and had
avenged his death.[13]   They were made prisoners
along with what was left of the detachment.
Part of it had escaped through the woods and
reached Fort de la Presque Isle.   The prisoners
were taken to New York.   When Captain Aubry
recovered, he was sent back to France,
remaining there until the peace of 1763.[14]   At
this time he was given command of six free companies of the marine maintained at New Orleans,
the capital of Louisiana, and immediately went
to that country.   When the Spaniards took possession of Louisiana, Captain Aubry, its former
governor, started back to France with his

---

de Villiers in this battle (PHC).
        The battle is called La Belle Famille.
The French force of marines, militia, and
Indians attacked the English in column due to
the topography.   The English had hastily
erected crude fortification and their fire
broke the French column.   In addition to Aubry,
Ligneris was also wounded and captured.   He
later died of his wounds.   Also captured was
Joseph Marin, a marine officer who was well
known for raiding behind English lines.
        [13]This was probably not Louis de Villiers
but rather Francois de Villiers.   Louis,
apparently, died of smallpox in late 1757.
        [14]By this peace, France ceded to Spain the
whole of Louisiana, and Captain Aubry was sent
there only to keep in order the French settlers
in the country who did not want to submit to
government nor to resign themselves to
dependence on Europe.   They were always
fighting against them (JCB).

troops. Their vessel, however, unluckily foun-
dered not far from the French port with all on
board. Such was the tragic end of this brave,
worthy, and wise officer.

The winter's amusements were such as I
have described before; balls, as well as races
on snow and ice, in sleighs and toboggans. In
the midst of these pleasures, marriage with a
young lady of a good family of fine enough con-
nections, but rather poor, was proposed to me.
Even her near relations approached me on the
subject. I refused, because I did not feel so
inclined, and because I thought this proposal
was made only because of the small fortune I
possessed. They plagued me, however, until I
finally gave my consent. Accordingly, I had
the folly to rent, temporarily, an entire
house; and added to this by spending ten thousand francs for furniture, and then lodging the
girl and her mother there, for the mother was a
widow. I had not told my friends about my
plans, but it was not long before they heard of
them. They tried to get me to break my promise, in several ways. My superior officers
remonstrated with me. Then, after hesitating
two months, I decided to break the engagement,
which indeed was only verbal. The problem of
getting my furniture back still remained. By
my carelessness, it was in the charge of the
mother and the daughter. It would not be easy
to get back; for I was informed that the family
had agreed to oppose this, considering my furniture an indemnity for my breech of promise.
I had to resort to a ruse, and succeeded in
taking it away by the authority of a court
order, with the help of my friends. Wishing to
show generosity in my actions, I left some
pieces of furniture in the house, paid the
rent, and gave them notice to leave. I found
that during the winter I had spent a total of
fifteen thousand francs, including the cost of
the furniture.

Word came the the enemy was preparing to
invade the heart of Canada in the next campaign, after the upper country had been

secured.   This caused preparations to be made
to withstand any attack they might undertake.

XIV

As reported by J.C.B., the French began to retreat toward central Canada, being pressed on all sides. With the destruction of Fort Duquesne at the end of the previous year, the English were able to besiege Fort Niagara. General Wolfe, due to the capture of Louisbourg, sailed with his army up the St. Lawrence unchallenged until he came to Quebec. General Amherst moved methodically up the Champlain Valley with an army so superior in numbers that the French had no alternative but to shorten their defensive lines by destroying Forts Carillon and St. Frederic (Crown Point) and taking a stand just south of Montreal. Thanks to J.C.B. being transferred from the southern front to the western front we get a picture of the activity in both areas.

Year 1759: At the beginning of March of this year, a levy of six hundred men, half of them regulars and half militia, was made at Quebec. I was again included in this number. Before I left that city, I set my affairs in order, giving and entrusting not only all my furniture and goods but also the sum of forty-five thousand francs in provincial paper money, to the integrity of an artillery sergeant. This man had a good reputation in Quebec where he was established. This amount was the greater part of my fortune, for I kept with me only ten francs in paper money.

The 18th of the same month, everything was ready for departure, and the detachment of six hundred men made a land march to Three Rivers. There we left two hundred men, intending to send them to Montreal. We then crossed to the southern side of the Saint Lawrence River, passing the Richelieu Islands at the western end of Lake St. Pierre near the River St. Francois where there is a rather populous vil-

lage of Abenaquis savages. This part of the
country has long been the stage for bloody
scenes of the Iroquois wars.

Fish are plentiful in the River St.
Francois. There are bass, gold fish, black
bass, and muskellunge. The last is a species
of pike which has a head larger than the common
pike, and a curved mouth under its nose which
gives it a singular appearance. We went on
from the Richelieu Islands to the River Sorel
above Lake St. Pierre.

This river was originally called the River
of the Iroquois, then the Richelieu, and
finally the Sorel. After we had gone fifteen
leagues up this river, we passed Chambly
Rapids. Above these rapids, there was a fort
of the same name but it had been destroyed.
From here we went on to Fort Sainte Therese and
Fort St. Jean, small and old forts that were
built for the wars against the Iroquois. They
no longer served any useful purpose, and were
abandoned. Then we entered Lake Champlain,
said to be at least fifty leagues long.

Everywhere we traveled along the route we
found, in addition to rivers teeming with fish,
all kinds of game animals in the woods. Among
others there is the moose, which is called elk
in Germany and Muscovy. In Canada, this animal
is the size of a horse. Its hindquarters are
large, its tail is as long as a man's middle
finger, and its haunches very high. It has
feet and legs like deer, and long hair covers
its neck and withers. Its head is about two
feet long, and this prolongation makes it look
wicked. Its muzzle is large, and the upper
part is slightly turned under like a camel's.
Its nostrils are big enough to thrust an arm
in. Its horns, flat and forked like a mule-
deers, are not much shorter than an elk's.
They shed and renew their horns each year. The
coat is a mixture of silver grey and red, and
thins out when the animal grows old. In the
country it is used to make mattresses and sad-
dles. Its flesh has a very good flavor, and is
nourishing but not heavy. The skin is very

soft and flexible, is used for chamois, and makes good buff leather.

The moose likes the cold country. In the summer it eats grass, and in winter it gnaws trees. When the snow is deep, the animals assemble in herds under the fir trees for shelter from the bad weather. Then it is easy to hunt them, but it is even easier in strong sunlight. When there is little snow, it is difficult and dangerous to get near a moose because, when wounded, it will become enraged and turn upon the hunter to trample him under its feet. The hunter can escape its fury by throwing his coat to the animal. The moose vents its rage on the coat, while the hunter, hiding behind a tree, can get ready to dispatch it.

The northern savages have another way of hunting this animal without any risk. They divide into two bands. One band gets in canoes and, joining in line, they form a half circle, each end touching the shore. The other band on shore makes a large circle and loose their dogs¹ to start up the moose enclosed in the area. The dogs chase the moose before them and force them to plunge into the water. No sooner are they in the water, then fire is opened upon them from all the canoes. They very rarely escape from such an attack.

The most terrible enemy of the moose is the cougar, a species of the cat family, whose tail is so long that it goes several times around its body. When it encounters a moose, it leaps upon it, seizes its neck, and severs the jugular vein. The only way a moose can escape this misfortune is by jumping into the water.

The savages consider the moose an animal which brings luck, and believe those who dream about them can expect long life. With the bear, it is just the opposite.

---

¹The dogs of the savages are all of the same variety, they somewhat resemble shepherd dogs, and have similar instincts (JCB).

The porcupine is also found in these parts. It is as large as an ordinary dog, but shorter and not so tall. Its bristles are about eight to ten inches long and as thick as a straw. These black and white bristles are very stiff, especially on the back. They form a weapon for both offense and defense. It darts them forth if it is approached; and no matter how slightly the bristles penetrate the flesh, they must be drawn out at once or they will sink all the way in (I am not sure of this fact, though the Canadians believe it is true). Great care is taken to keep the dogs from going too near them. The flesh of the porcupine is good to eat, especially when turned on a spit. It is as good as a milk-fed pig.

When we had sailed the length of Lake Champlain, we found the site of the Fort of Point a la Chevelure, which the English destroyed after the defeat of the French army led by Baron de Dieskau. At this place they found only twenty-five men, whom they took prisoners.[2] Not far from this site is located Fort Carillon, which the English call Ticonderoga. We were bound for this post, the last French post in this sector, because it was threatened by the English at Fort George only four leagues away. Here, the French led by General Montcalm had forced them to capitulate and withdraw the previous year; nevertheless, they had returned to it and fortified them- selves. At the time of our arrival, there were only two hundred and fifty men under the com- mand of General Bourlamarque in the garrison at Fort Carillon. Our reinforcement increased it by one hundred and fifty, not enough to hold this important post. We remained there very quietly for about two months. During this time, the commander had laid mines under the fort and bastions to blow up the whole struc-

---

[2]As before noted, the English did not take Crown Point after Dieskau's defeat (PHC).

ture, it he found it necessary to abandon it.
This was not a useless precaution.

The 18th of June, the enemy came in sight
of the fort.[3] First their sharpshooters
advanced to give the body of the army time to
erect six batteries. We returned their fire
from the trenches, still intact from the time
when General Montcalm had stopped twenty-two
thousand men and forced them to retreat. We
exchanged fire for three days; but when the
general saw the enemy batteries had been set
up, he did not want to undergo a siege in which
the enemy strength would overcome him, not
wishing to have himself and the garrison made
prisoners of war.[4]

Quietly in the darkness of the night of
June 26th, he had the men of the garrison
embark in bateaux, with the exception of only
ten men, who were, an hour after the order was
given, to fire the trains of gunpowder leading
to the heaps of open powder barrels in the
mines already contrived for that purpose.

When the garrison had embarked, they had
to pass under the enemy's cannon. Despite the
fact they had been warned, for their own protection, to be quiet, they could not avoid
being heard because of the oars. This made the
enemy suspect something, and fire several cannon shots in their direction, but none of the
boats were hit, because the cannon was aimed
too high or probably not aimed at all in the
darkness. The firing did not cease, however,
until the enemy saw the explosion of the fort.
It was only then that they realized it had been
evacuated. English soldiers were then sent
into the fort, where they found eight of the
ten men we had left to blow up the fortifica-

---

[3]General Amherst set out from Fort George,
July 21, 1759. Bourlamarque escaped from
Ticonderoga on July 23, leaving a small force
which blew up and evacuated the fort on July 26
(PHC).

[4]He had orders to retire (PHC).

tion.   These eight were taken prisoners, but
the other two escaped, after carrying out their
task, to rejoin us about ten leagues away at
the Isle aux Noix,[5] where we had halted to
await the enemy and delay his advance toward
the vicinity of Montreal, now undermanned by
the French.   We obstructed the river with
stones and wooden stakes, at least to delay the
enemy's passage if we could not prevent it.
The two men, who had escaped from the fort and
rejoined us the morning after the explosion,
told us that only one of the bastions had not
been destroyed because the mine had been inef-
fective.   The other mines had operated satis-
factorily.

I was sent out on the 28th with another
man to blow up Fort Sainte Therese and Fort St.
Jean, which I have mentioned before.   We accomplished our task[6] to the satisfaction of the
general, who had entrenched himself on the Isle
aux Noix to wait for the enemy, without intending to meet him in battle.   His sole intention
was to delay their march, falling back as they
advanced, which he was not to do until he had
received further orders.

In Quebec, as well as Montreal, it was
well known that there was an English fleet in
the lower reaches of the River St. Lawrence.[7]
This fleet was coming upstream with a landing
force to besiege Quebec.   Our task was, therefore, to get into a position to oppose this
enterprise, as well as to thwart any attempt

---

[5]An island in the river below the lake
(PHC).

[6]Major Robert Rogers found Fort St. Jean
and Fort Ste. Therese manned and alert in June
of 1760.   He took Fort Ste. Therese.   It is
possible that the French had reconstructed
fortifications at these sites as Rogers says
that the fort he took was a small stockade
(Rogers 1966:183-184).

[7]Wolfe's fleet sailed from Louisbourg June
6, and sighted Quebec June 21 (PHC).

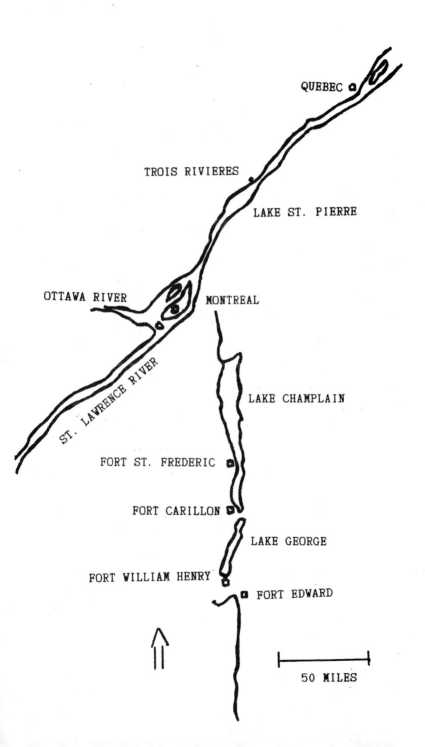

the enemy might make at other points in the country. This motive kept General Bourlamarque at the post on Isle aux Noix, where he might watch the enemy's army coming into the heart of Canada. The upper country was still to be defended. All the forts, as far away as Fort Duquesne, were in the enemy's power, no longer being able to hold back an invasion. It was decided to send a detachment, with an engineer, above the rapids to build a fort.

July 4th, I was sent with another man from Isle aux Noix to Montreal to take twelve cannons to Isle Levis, the most remote of the three Isles of Galots (mentioned before). Isle Levis is two leagues this side of La Galette. When we reached Montreal and made known the object of our visit, we were entrusted with transporting the artillery, which consisted of six six-pounders and six twelve-pounders. They were quickly loaded into bateaux, manned by sixty men, which contained munitions and provisions. All this was directed by an officer.

We left Montreal July 12th, passed the rapids in short stages, and reached Isle Levis on the 24th. We found the fort half-finished, because of the pains taken by an engineer Desaudroins, who had come from France with General Montcalm. Our first care was to unload our cannons. This fort was not completed until the end of September. It was built of squared wooden timbers covered with earth, six feet thick, and had three bastions of four cannons each. The bastions were connected by a parapet three feet wide. There was a drawbridge at the entrance, with three buildings and some casements inside the bastions. Outside, they built breastworks four and a half feet high, and brushwood was piled very thickly to prevent the enemy from making an easy landing, in case an entrance was attempted there.

When I arrived at this post, the engineer employed me as his secretary, making me at the same time superintendent of laborers. My compensation for these positions was two hundred piastres a month. Scarcely two weeks after my arrival at this post, I was informed that the

artillery commander had appointed me sergeant
of the second company of gunners. I declined
this position, because I should get more annoy-
ance than profit from it. I could earn much
more on my trips, without undergoing such rigid
discipline.

While we were still working in the construction of Fort Levis, news came of the fall
of Quebec.

The English fleet, mentioned before when
it was in the lower St. Lawrence River, moved
up on the 20th of June to a point of the Island
of Orleans, where it might be seen from Quebec.
The fleet numbered thirty sails, and had
remained in the lower reaches of the river for
about a month prior to this time.[8]

No sooner had the English anchored within
sight of the city, than every colonist took up
arms to defend this colonial capital. General
Montcalm made every attempt to oppose the enemy's attack. He began by sending out eight
fire ships he had caused to be built to set
fire to the hostile fleet; but the men in
charge of the foray acted too hastily, because
of fear, or for some other reason. As a
result, the enemy saw the danger, and promptly
avoided it to save their fleet.

When he saw that his plan had failed,
General Montcalm went to Quebec on the other
side of the St. Charles River, on the Beauport
shore, where the enemy might easily land, and
where they had made some unsuccessful attempts
to that end. At last, on the first of July,
the enemy fleet lifted anchor and sailed into
the harbor directly opposite the city. The
French immediately fired upon them; thereupon,
the English began a bombardment of both the
upper and lower towns.[9] The latter was almost

---

[8]An English fleet had been crusing in the
Gulf of St. Lawrence to intercept French supply
ships before Wolfe's fleet arrived (PHC).

[9]Wolfe occupied Point Levis, and bombarded
the town from that position (PHC).

entirely burned and destroyed, while the upper
town was also damaged.

Every family had left the city, withdraw-
ing four leagues into the country. All had
temporarily packed there furniture and belongings into strong cellars to protect them
against fire. General Montcalm still guarded
the Beauport shore with part of the regular and
militia forces, because he suspected that the
enemy's intention was to make a feint against
the city, in order that actually they might
land more easily on the shore when the French
left their entrenchments. Such, however, did
not prove to be the English intention. They
continued the siege for two months and a half
without any success other than destroying the
lower city and badly damaging the upper city.
Becoming impatient at the duration of the
siege, the enemy decided to attempt a landing,
which was accomplished on September 13th, an
hour before daybreak, with six thousand men
commanded by General Wolfe.[10]

General Wolfe's forces landed a league
from the city, in a place called Anse des
Meres,[11] where care had been taken to place a
strong outpost commanded by a captain named
Vergor,[12] but this guard allowed itself to be
surprised. The foe then was free to move up
and blockade the city by land, as well as cut
off any outside aid that might have reached it.

---

[10]This is the same man who besieged
Louisbourg in the preceding year (JCB).

[11]This is identified as the Anse de Foulon
in most sources.

[12]Louis du Pont de Chambon, Sieur de
Vergor was a captain in the French army who
came to Canada as a captain of marines. He was
the commandant of Fort Beausejour when it
surrendered in 1755 under circumstances so
questionable that he was court-martialed. He
was acquitted, perhaps due to his association
with Intendant Bigot's group.

No sooner had General Montcalm heard this news than he left Beauport with the four thousand men he commanded to go to the relief of the city. Wolfe's army, on the watch, saw the French and advanced to meet them on the Plains of Abraham, which face the St. Charles River half a league from the city. The English were drawn up in battle order on this hill, awaiting the French who, at a forced march, were coming up the same side through the upper valley of the St. Charles River to fight the enemy. When the French reached the foot of this declivity, they had to scale these heights. This they did with great courage and spirit, displaying the true impetuosity of the French.

Upon reaching the top, the French, led by their general, fired two successive volleys at the enemy; one of which mortally wounded General Wolfe, the English commander. His men immediately carried him away, and he died the same day. After the second volley, the English charged with fixed bayonets. The French resisted stubbornly. General Montcalm received two wounds; one received in the abdomen, while charging the enemy, proved to be fatal. He was taken to Quebec, after urging his soldiers to endeavor to maintain the honor of France. There he died the next day, and was buried in a shell hole in the Ursuline convent on the Rue Saint Louis.[13]

The loss of this battle by the French, meant the capture of Quebec, which held out four days more, and finally surrendered on September 17th to General Murray, the successor of General Wolfe.

The remainder of the French army which had fought on the Plains of Abraham, had withdrawn into the hills since they could not enter Quebec. Ten leagues from the city, they met another French army, commanded by General Levis

---

[13]Montcalm, born in Condiac, was of the same Rouergue family as Gozon, grand master of the Isle of Rhodes (JCB).

who was coming to relieve Quebec. When he
learned of General Montcalm's death and the
defeat of Montcalm's army, Levis surmised that
the city had surrendered, and thought it wise
not to advance farther, but to entrench himself
to hold back the foe in case they should try to
capture more of the county. For this reason,
he made camp and prepared to march in full
force upon Quebec the following spring; either
to besiege the city or to take it by surprise
attack.

Montcalm's defeat had alarmed the rest of
the country. No longer was a strong defense
possible, since we had no more cities or
strongholds, and no more heavy artillery.

If the country was worried, personally I
was even more disturbed. All my property was
in Quebec, and I did not know whether it had
been saved or had fallen a prey to the enemy or
possibly destroyed by fire. I was at a post
one hundred and ten leagues from Quebec, so I
could get no news of its fate. I had to make
up my mind to wait and remain uncertain. I
still had twelve thousand francs of provincial
money with me to which I might add the salary
of the two positions I held; but still there
remained my fear that the entire country might
be conquered.

The city of Quebec had previously been
taken by the English, first in 1629, and given
back in 1632, as told at the beginning of these
travels. It was attacked again in 1690 by an
English fleet, which had to raise the siege
because the Iroquois did not give them the help
they had promised, and did not even come to
meet them. In 1710, another English fleet
appeared in the St. Lawrence River with a landing force of six thousand men; but part of this
fleet was lost, and the city was again saved.[14]

The year 1759 was not fortunate for
Canada, for the French met with a succession of
setbacks. Fort Duquesne, in the upper country,

---

[14]The year should be 1711 (PHC).

had been evacuated because of the fall of Fort
Presque Isle.[15] Its garrison, no longer able
to get through, had to retire to Louisiana.[16]
The garrison of Presque Isle retreated north-
ward to Michilimackinac, while that of Niagara
fell back to Montreal,[17] as did the Fort
Frontenac garrison. As a result, the French
now held in the upper country nothing more than
Fort Levis and the small post of La Galette,
two leagues beyond, which had a garrison of
only fifteen men. In the south of Canada there
was no stronghold except the five hundred men
commanded by General Bourlamarque.

With the fall of Quebec, the English held
all the keys to the country. Only the heart of
Canada remained to be conquered, and the enemy
would not find that very difficult to accom-
plish. They would, however, find it necessary
to actually conquer it, for the French were
determined to dispute every inch of ground,
giving up only when forced to do so. At Fort
Levis, where I was stationed, all was quiet
during the rest of the campaign; but we were
very certain that such would not be the case
during the following year.

---

[15]Fort Duquesne was abandoned in November,
1758, because of the approach of a strong
English force under General John Forbes. The
capture of Fort Niagara by Sir William Johnson
in July 1759, forced the French in northwestern
Pennsylvania to flee to Detroit (PHC).

Aside from the threat of Forbes' army and
the Indians remaining neutral, an English force
captured Fort Frontenac in 1758 and destroyed
the supplies meant for Fort Duquesne and the
boats that were to carry them. This may be the
incident that J.C.B. refers to as the fall of
Fort Presque Isle.

[16]Part went up the Allegheny River to Fort
Machault (Franklin); part went to the Illinois
country (PHC).

[17]The Niagara garrison capitulated to the
English (PHC).

XV

*J.C.B.'s report of the siege of Fort Levis
seems unemotional. The English bombardment of
this fort was intense and the threat of reprisals for the attack on the survivors of Fort
William Henry was in the back of the minds of
the French. England's Iroquois allies where
just a liable to kill the wounded and prisoners
as would the French Indian allies.*

Year 1760: The 6th of January, the campaign began with the capture of the post of La
Galette. The fifteen men in garrison there
were made prisoners.

We were then confined on our island without a single savage to send out to reconnoiter.
No news reached us except that coming from
Montreal, where all the French forces were
massed after the fall of Quebec.

May 23, a courier brought word that
General Bourlamarque and his detachment had
retreated from Isle aux Noix to join forces
with General Levis, commander in chief after
the death of the Marquis de Montcalm. On the
16th of April, these commanders left together,
at the head of an army corps made up of all
regular and militia troops available for service. They made a land and water journey to
recapture Quebec. When they came near the
city, the detachment coming by water was on the
point of attacking a large enemy force of fifteen hundred men stationed three leagues from
Quebec. This guard would undoubtedly have been
captured or cut to pieces, had not an unexpected incident occurred. Just as two gunners
were landing, they fell into the water. One
was drowned and the other, clinging to a cake
of ice, climbed upon it and was carried away by
the current. The ice cake, drifting down-
stream, grazed the shore of the lower city. A
sentinel saw this man and called for help. The

English immediately went to seize the poor wretch, who was found unconscious. He was recognized by his uniform and carried to the governor's house, where they restored him to consciousness with spirituous liquors. Then, when questioned, he said just before he died that an army of ten thousand men was very near. The English general, Murray, immediately sent orders to have the outposts retreat with all possible speed.

Although this order was sent, it arrived only at the moment when the English outpost was attacked by the French, who pursued the enemy, after defeating and killing many of their men. But fatigue and cold halted the French, who had to camp and start fires to get warm. General Murray at once sallied forth from Quebec, with four thousand men and some artillery, to face the French in their encampment. He approached the camp, and raked it with a volley of musketry. This forced the French to extinguish their fires. The enemy then discontinued firing because of the darkness of the night. But they remained near by until daybreak, at which time the French charged with fixed bayonets so fiercely that the English fell back and were pursued up to the gates of the city, losing their artillery, and eight hundred men, killed in action.[1]

The French would undoubtedly have entered the city on the heels of the enemy if the entire French army had been equally zealous in pursuit. The small number of pursuers, however, did not dare to go into Quebec alone after the enemy, and remained on the slope of the walls awaiting the rest of the army, which did not come up until an hour had elapsed. They were put to work digging trenches, work that was difficult because they had to be cut out of rock.

---

[1] This battle took place near Sillery and Ste. Foy.

Unfortunately, we had no field pieces. Nevertheless, we besieged the city from April 27th to May 16th, because we hoped that help would arrive from France; but none ever came. The siege would have lasted longer if the enemy had not decided to have part of the fleet sail back up the river. This made the French apprehensive of being caught between two fires, with retreat cut off. So they had to raise the siege and retreat to Montreal, the chief base where the French forces were reunited. There was indeed the city of Three Rivers, half way to Montreal; but it had no defenses, and the small garrison there received orders to fall back to Montreal when the enemy approached.

During the pursuit of the enemy to the gates of Quebec, General Bourlamarque, who led the French charge, had three horses killed under him. The third horse was hit in the chest by a cannon ball, the same ball carrying away the calf of this brave officers right leg, the surprising fact being his boot was undamaged. The general, despite his wound, did not cease commanding. Were it not for his wound, it was believed that General Bourlamarque would have entered the city with the enemy, so much confidence in him did his soldiers have, which proves that a good general makes good soldiers.

This setback for the French made it apparent that all of Canada soon would be in English hands.

June 6, a detachment of one hundred and fifty men under Captain Pouchot[2] came to Fort Levis to reinforce its garrison. In this way, the effective force was raised to three hundred and seventy-five men. When this captain

---

[2]The same man was commander at Niagara when it was taken on June 26, 1756 (JCB). Actually, he was commander at Niagara when it was taken in July, 1759 (PHC).

Pouchot had done an earlier tour (before 1759) at Niagara. He was sent there to improve the fortifications.

arrived, he took command and appointed me his
secretary. At once, he put me in charge of the
powder magazine. Word came that an English
army was to come through the upper country to
join forces with the army at Quebec and the
central army. They were to meet at Montreal.
Accordingly, we took measures for defense to
hinder this junction as much as we could. For
this purpose, we had two small sailboats two
leagues above Fort Levis at the entrance to
Lake Ontario. These two sailboats usually
plied between Fort Niagara and the fort of La
Galette; but after the capture of these posts
they were no longer in use. It was decided to
place them as guard ships, so that they could
warn Fort Levis by three cannon shots as soon
as the enemy came in sight.

When on the 16th of August the enemy
appeared, the two boats, of course, fired the
three cannon shots as signal. but an hour
later they were surrounded by several gunboats,
which despite their resistance forced the
French to strike their flags. The English
seized them and compelled the crews to sail up
to fire on the fort. This was carried out at
once. Fort Levis then returned fire. One of
these boats, already badly damaged, ran aground
a league farther down. The other boat, which
did not retreat, was riddled with bullets, and
ran aground in front of the fort. The fire
from the fort was unceasing upon the boat and
upon the enemy army which was filing along the
shore to the north, losing not less than three
bateaux and several men.

After the entire army had passed, they
came to set up batteries on the island nearest
the fort. They even attempted a landing on our
island, but without success. They then began a
cannonade and bombardment on the 18th, and kept
it up without interruption until the 25th.
During this time, one bastion was destroyed and
three gunners killed. Finally, on the 25th,
Commander Pouchot, realizing further resistance
would be futile, began at daybreak to fire
salutes from the cannons as long as the powder
lasted, doing this to use up the rest of the

war munitions.   This astonished the enemy, who
had no other thought than that it was the
birthday of the King of France, which was actually that day, and the French were really not
much concerned if they were thus celebrating.
But they were mistaken; for the real purpose
was to use up all the ammunition so that the
enemy would not profit by it.   At ten o'clock
in the morning, the firing ceased and the flag
was lowered.   Then the enemy sent us an officer
with a flag of truce.   We agreed with him on
the terms of the capitulation, which were that
the garrison would march out next morning with
the honors of war, then ground their arms, and
be taken prisoners to New York, where they
would remain.

    At eight o'clock next morning, we left the
fort, as had been agreed the evening before.
We were kept under guard for two hours, while
they inspected the fort.   The enemy with a
force of ten thousand men commanded by General
Amherst,[3] was astonished that such a small
force held out so long and prevented their
attempt to land.   The enemy general could not
keep from praising the French, with the remark
that he was surprised that more men had not
been killed, since he had partially destroyed
the fort.   Actually, during the siege, we lost
only fourteen men; and we had only thirty-five
wounded, twelve of whom remained in the fort,
unable to march out with us.   It is true that
we lost sixteen on the two boats which the
enemy seized.   We had as a result, at the time
of the capitulation, only three hundred and
thirty-three men, twenty-three of them wounded.
The enemy lost fifty-six men.

---

    [3]The same general was at the siege of
Louisbourg with General Wolfe in June, 1758
(JCB).

XVI

The surrender of Fort Levis opened the western approach to Montreal, the last bastion of French Canada. General Murray, having suffered through a hard winter and a short siege in Quebec, brought the English forces from the east. The attempt to hold in the south was abandoned. The fortifications at Montreal were inadequate. After the usual formalities, the city, and Canada, surrendered.

On the 27th, we were embarked in boats, escorted by fifty men. We went to the south of Lake Ontario as far as the River de Chouaguin (Oswego River in English), and then followed its course for thirty leagues. This river is full of rapids and falls, one of them about ten foot high. At the end of the river we came to the fort of Onoyotes, later called Oneidas by the English. A league beyond it, we entered the lake of the same name. This lake is seven leagues long, and at its end there is a river whose name I have forgotten, but which has a dam halfway up. Fort Stanwix[1] is located ten leagues beyond. Next is a meadow where we saw Fort Johnson.[2] The Corlac River is six leagues farther, and beyond it is Albany on the Hudson River. There we were put on board some small sailboats which took us to New York, which we reached on the 20th of September. When I landed, I went to lodge with the others in the house allotted to us. We were free to leave it as we pleased, to walk about the city and its surroundings. The house was situated at the end of the Place d'Armes, and faced the harbor.

---

[1] Rome, New York. There may have been a French fort at this site as early as 1689.
[2] Home of Sir William Johnson.

This city, rectangular in shape, is in a fine location on the end of Manhattan Island. The island is three leagues long and one league wide. It is bounded on the northwest by the Hudson River, whose mouth is two miles away, and bounded on the east by the long island, called Long Island in English, which is separated from it by only a small sea inlet, half a league long. Long Island is thirty leagues long and four wide. According to the census 1760, New York had twenty-five thousand inhabitants of diverse nationalities and creeds. The beginning of its building was with wooden cabins in 1609. In the following year, the Dutch, who were the first inhabitants, built it under the name New Belgium. In 1614, they gave it the name of New Holland. When the Swedes took this city in 1638, they named it New Sweden. Retaken by the Dutch in 1655, it resumed the name New Holland. When the English seized it in 1664, they renamed it New Jersey, and later New York, which last name it has retained.[3]

This city has only one fine street, in the center of which they have market and butcher's stalls. Most of the houses on this street are of brick. This is the street I have called the "grand plaza."[4] On the other streets the houses are of wood.

The state of New York has a narrow stretch of three or four leagues on the seaboard. About twelve leagues inland, it widens gradually and extends to the north. The Hudson River rises in the Appalachian or Allegheny Mountains, which start between Lake George (called Lake Saint Sacrement by the French) and Lake Ontario. These mountains extend as far as Carolina, and separate Canada from New England.

---

[3] It is hardly necessary to say that this summary of New York's history is full of errors. Henry Hudson visited Hudson River in 1609. New Amsterdam, later New York, was founded in 1626 (PHC).

[4] Broadway (PHC).

The Hudson river floats only light boats at first for twenty-two leagues. Even this navigation is broken by cascades. It is not very easily navigated again until near Albany, fifty-three leagues from New York. There, it is only about fifty leagues from the sea.

The day after my arrival in New York, I met two French prisoners who had been there a month, boarding at their own expense at an inn on Broadway. These two men, with whom I had been acquainted, invited me to live with them. I was favorable, but before making a decision, I thought it time to take stock of my assets.

I had brought with me only thirteen thousand five hundred francs in Canadian paper money. This was all I possessed. I had, indeed, a gold watch, some shoe buckles and garters, as well as some solid-gold collar buttons and cuff links. I thought of selling them, but the amount I would get from them could not support me very long. Therefore, I decided to sell part of my paper money. The English readily bought it, but their price was low. I finally agreed to sell the greater part of my paper, giving a five hundred franc note for ten guineas. This was selling my paper at the low rate of two and one-half per cent. This sacrifice was less distressing for me than the sale of my watch and other belongings I have listed above. I had just given these up for five guineas, because I thought the paper worthless. Nevertheless, I kept four thousand paper francs as a last resource in an emergency.

With my fifteen guineas, I went to stay at the inn where my two compatriots were. The innkeeper was a Frenchman, who served very good meals, three days a week in the French style, and the rest of the week in English style, all table d'hote. My expense for room and board was three shillings a day. Only red beer was served at the table; there was an extra charge for wine.

A few days later, we learned of the complete surrender of Canada. The three English armies, mentioned above, met before Montreal;

and, on September 8th, demanded the surrender of the city. In several days' time the French generals were forced back and driven into the city. Since they could not hold out against three army corps, they decided to capitulate. General Bourlamarque, however, thought the capitulation was dishonorable, and refused to sign it. Only Generals Levis and de Bougainville[5] did so. The French marched out of the city with the honors of war, but were held prisoner and shipped to Quebec. They were to stay there until the following spring, when they would be sent to Europe.

I will mention here an incident that occurred before the fall of Montreal. It was five days after General Murray and his fleet had sailed from Quebec into actual sight of Montreal. He was waiting impatiently for General Amherst's army, and decided to send out a spy. This spy was a Canadian, a rather ill-favored, misshapen fellow, which is unusual among the people of this country, who are ordinarily well built. This man went alone in a small canoe to the French camp, half a league from the city. He stopped at a tent, asked for food, and made several inquiries. Among other things, he asked how many men were in the French army. His bold manner and his questions aroused suspicion among the soldiers he was talking to. As they did not answer, he moved on to another tent where he had no better luck. Finally he went to a third tent where he asked the same questions. A suspicious soldier who had followed him heard him make these similar

---

[5]After the return of these generals to France, General Levis was made Marshal of France. M. de Bourlamarque was sent to relieve Malta, and on his return was sent to Guadeloupe, where he died. M. de Bougainville devoted himself to navigation, made some discoveries, and after several voyages became a Senator and Member of the Institute of France (JCB).

inquiries, and told his sergeant about it. The
sergeant questioned this fellow, and found his
replies suspicious. Then he had him watched,
without his knowledge, and went to inform
General Bourlamarque, who had the man brought
before him. He questioned him, and suspecting
he was a spy, the general ordered him stripped
and searched. When he found nothing in his
clothing, they took of his shoes, and found in
the end of his stockings two small unsealed
letters, bent by the shoes. The general read
them. They were messages to General Amherst,
urging him to hurry his advance and make a land
blockade of the city, and stating that they
were expecting his arrival to begin the siege
at the day and hour mentioned. At sight of
these letters General Bourlamarque became certain of the espionage and ordered the man hung,
which was done at once..

Despite her resistance, Canada was
entirely subdued after eight years of war in
the interior. After the English had at first
fought for four years in the upper country for
their trade and boundaries, they finally went
on to invade the colony. The French resisted
with courage and daring, though always inferior
in number. The loss of Canada was a loss for
France, which seemingly was unaware of its
value. The whole country was exploited for the
sole profit of the officials who were sent
there. This will be evident later in the trial
of the last officials sent over, whose prede-
cessors had deserved similar treatment.

Why, however, had the French government
neglected to send the help which was asked for
repeatedly? They knew how much this colony
needed it. Beyond a doubt, it is probable that
a reinforcement of six thousand more men at the
proper time could have defeated all the
attempts of the English; could have done them
much damage; and saved the colony. It is no
less true that Canada, with her feeble forces,
made a valiant defense, and disputed every foot
of soil with the enemy so heroically that it
seemed out of the ordinary. This even the
English conceded. It was, then, either indif-

ference or policy which made France neglect to
send any considerable reinforcement to this
colony, because it cost her more than she
received from it. But if, several years before
the war, trustworthy investigators had been
sent to find out the reason for this state of
affairs, it would inevitably have been discovered how the governors, the intendants, the
treasurers, the commissary generals, and other
officials who owed their positions to influence
alone, succeeded in getting rich. Then the
government would have profited by the wealth of
the country, and would not have been obliged to
prosecute the last officials.

In the second place, France has lost
rather than gained. The shameful peace of 1763
proves this by her willingness to give up
Canada. She lost a profitable trade in furs,
three hundred cannons, and even had to pay out
several millions, both to the English for
expenses of various prisoners they had taken,
and to the bearers of colonial paper money, who
had bought it at a low price and were now paid
at face value. Since this cession, the English
have been more clever in exploiting the prod-
ucts of Canada.

The extent of this vast country is not yet
determined. It is believed to be larger than
half of Europe, and that it would require one
hundred forty million inhabitants to populate
it as densely as New England (now the United
States). The greater part of Canada consists
of vast swamps. forests and woods, lakes and
rivers. At the time it was taken, there were
no more than eighty thousand inhabitants, not
counting the savages, whose number is unknown.[6]

---

[6]In 1760, it was estimated that there were
only eighty-six tribes scattered in the various
villages, as follows: in lower Canada,
including Acadia, twelve; in the north, forty;
in the south, ten; and twenty-four between the
Ohio and Louisiana. Figuring a thousand men to
a tribe, we get eighty-six thousand fighting

Before the discovery of Canada, the forests which covered it were but one vast haunt
of wild beasts. They had multiplied extraordi-
narily because there were few men frequenting
these wilds, and the absence of domestic animals left more room and more food for the various wild and roving species, as well as for the
savages themselves. But this host of animals
was subject to man's dominion, which included
every living thing. Without knowledge of the
arts or of agriculture, the savages got food
and clothing solely at the expense of the
beasts. When the European fashion adopted the
use of skins, the American savages slaughtered
them more vigorously because it obtained for
them an abundance of new possessions, and more
murderously because they had adopted our firearms. This industry of slaughter sent a great
quantity of furs and skins from the forests of
Canada to the ports of France. A part of these
were used in the kingdom, and the rest in the
neighboring states. Most of these furs were
known in Europe, which used to get them from
the north of the European hemisphere, but the
amount was too small to permit a very extensive
use of them. Whim and fancy had made them more
or less fashionable ever since the interest in
the colonies and America had begun to gain
favor for them in the mother country. This
fact is judiciously explained by Raynal in his
History of the Two Indies.

While making these reflections on the loss
of Canada, I do not overlook my personal loss.
I have said before that I had begun by losing
my trunk which contained, besides my belongings, the sum of ten thousand francs; that
since then I had left in a warehouse at Quebec
various pieces of furniture and other belongings with forty-five thousand francs in provincial money. After spending fifteen thousand
francs during the winter of 1758-1759, I had
subsequently earned eighty thousand francs, not

---

men (JCB).

counting the thirteen thousand five hundred francs that I had taken to New York. Of all my property I had only to regret what was left in Quebec. I saw no way of recovering it without going back, which would not be easy for me as a prisoner of war. I had to make up my mind to wait until I reached France and then find out, through persons returning from the colony, whether I had lost all my belongings or could hope to recover something.

In 1758, I had indeed decided to convert my provincial money into bills of exchange on the Treasurer of the French Marine Office; but this was not possible, for an order had come forbidding persons to draw on it any more. The reason for this was that a large amount had already been drawn, on which payment was stopped because there was a suspicion of corruption or at least maladministration. This was well-founded, as will be shown.

Paper money was first introduced into Canada in 1670, to the amount of only one hundred thousand francs. In 1706, this issue of paper was increased to six hundred and fifty thousand francs, and a few years later withdrawn. In 1726, it was reissued in a different form—that is, on cards with values of ninety-six francs, forty-eight francs, twenty-four francs, twelve francs, six francs, three livres, thirty sous, fifteen sous, and seven sous six deniers. Each card had the arms of France stamped on it, and was signed personally by the governor, intendant, and treasurer. The amount in circulation was only eight hundred thousand francs. In 1748, besides these cards, there were introduced paper drafts, worth from twenty sous to a hundred francs and signed the intendant alone. As a result, the whole quantity of paper money increased in 1751 to only three millions; but the war situation together with the monopoly held by intriguing officials, caused it, at the time the colony was lost, to reach eighty millions more than the government had authorized. This was the reason the payment of bills of exchange was suspended until the cause of this extraordinary increase was discovered.

When the officials who had shared in the administration returned to France after the cession of Canada, they went with minds at ease. They had no idea that the government would make any investigation, for it had given no sign of its intentions. Nineteen of them were arrested and sent to the Bastille. Then a commission was appointed with De Sartine, lieutenant-general of the police, as president. The trial lasted eighteen months, and the final decision reduced the entire debt to thirty-six millions. Eight of the embezzlers were ordered to make restitution of eleven millions, and were ordered punished by banishment, confiscation, and fines. The others were discharged, as they had turned state's evidence.

XVII

Returning to the subject of my stay in New York, I spent my money without doing anything except to visit the city and its surroundings.

I have said before that this city is populated by various sects. The variety of churches, which tolerance has permitted to be erected to the Divinity, makes an interesting sight in the city where each sect has its own church. Most astonishing is the fact that Quakers, Anabaptists, Dumplers,[1] Anglicans, Presbyterians, Methodists, Moravians, Lutherans, and Calvinists all pray to God beside each other, each in his own way, without troubling the good will that should prevail among citizens.

The Anabaptists,[2] who have the doctrine of community goods and lawfulness of a person's station in life (?), have no communion whatever with the other sects. They engage in prophesying; carry no arms for self-defense; and swear no oaths, except by yes and no. This sect, it is said, was the origin of the sect of Quakers,[3] who resemble them, share their humanitarianism, temperance, and chastity, and believe themselves inspired.

---

[1] Probably Dunkards (PHC).

[2] This sect rose in Germany in 1523. It was headed by Stork and Mundler, disciples of Luther. In 1534, John of Leyden, the successor of the original leaders, had himself made King by the sect. He died on the scaffold, January 2, 1536 (JCB).

[3] The sect of Quakers started in England in 1640. George Fox was their founder and leader. Five hundred of them settled in Pennsylvania, which was founded by William Penn, who was granted it by Charles II, in 1681 (JCB).

The Dumplers live apart, always reflecting and meditating. Men and women occupy separate quarters, meeting only in churches, and never assemble except for the business of the community. Their lives are made up of work, sleep, and prayer. Twice during the day and twice at night, they meet to pray. As is the case of the Quakers and the Methodists, everyone has the right to preach. The subjects of their discourses are humility, temperance, chastity, and other virtues. They believe in Heaven and Hell; but reject eternal damnation. The doctrine of original sin is an ungodly blasphemy to them, and they only baptize adults. They are indifferent to injuries, and can be deceived and mistreated without fear of retaliation or complaint. The men and women wear long white robes with hoods. Because of abstinence, they live only on roots and sleep on planks. All the fruits of their labor are shared by the community. They marry young or not at all. The newly-married must go to the country until they have had a child, then return.

I say nothing of the Anglicans, Presbyterians, Methodists, Moravians, Lutherans, and Calvinists, because their religious principles are generally known.

At New York, they decided to send the French prisoners out of the city. Consequently, on September 25th, several of us were sent to Jamaica on Long Island, four leagues from New York, where we were quartered at various places. I was sent to a miller's at Ahstide, where I stayed alone for a week, poorly fed, and unable to understand English. I found the time passed very slowly, and decided to try to return to New York. The prisoners were forbidden to leave their domiciles, and the sheriffs[4] were ordered to arrest

----

[4]Officers of justice who carry a white stick and have the right to arrest malefactors and lawbreakers (JCB).

and take to jail any prisoners on the highways
or away from their usual residence. The prisoners could not pretend ignorance of this
order, because they had been notified about it.
I decided at all events to ask my host to lend
me a horse. He hesitated but, at my insis-
tence, he gave in. The next morning, October
10th, I set out on the road. I had hardly gone
a league when I saw two riders trotting towards
me. I was uncertain whether to go on or go
back; but, thinking the risk would be the same
in any case, I decided to go on and take a
chance on my horse, whose strength I knew, as
soon as the two men approached me so that I
could not avoid them. The next moment one
tried to get ahead of me, and the other to get
behind. Then, spurring my horse, I soon out-
distanced the two men, who were actually sheriffs.

I continued on my way at top speed until I
reached Jamaica. I stopped on the way in, at a
place where two French prisoners that I knew
were staying. I begged them to put my horse in
the stable as soon as possible, and to say
nothing, as I was being followed by two sheriffs. Five minutes afterward, these two came
by, inquiring at the different houses if a man
on horseback had been seen passing. No one
could give them any information as I had
stopped on the way in, and no one could have
seen me except the people in the house I had
entered. An hour later on their way back, the
two men again went by the house where I was. I
had dinner with my two compatriots, and then
mounted my horse to go to the end of Long
Island. When I arrived there, I stabled my
horse at an inn and crossed to New York immediately. I reached the city toward evening, and
went to lodge at the inn where I had stayed
before.

The next day, I went to find Captain
Pouchot, with whom I had been taken prisoner
and with whom I had served as secretary. Two
motives took me to see this officer. The first
was to return the silver pencil he had lent me
for continuing my journal on our way to New

York. My other motive was to borrow some money. He seemed surprised to see me, knowing I had been sent six leagues from New York. I told him about the stratagem I had used to reach him. After this story, I spoke of my wish to stay in New York, and to find some occupation there, asking him to use his influence to help me. He did not seem to think it would be easy, since I could neither speak nor write English. But I had been informed that the English commissioner he lived with had as his secretary a French prisoner who had no better command of English than I, and moreover was a drunkard, this being a fault I had always despised. My officer, therefore, promised to speak for me. He said he would willingly do so, but could not promise that he would be successful. However, he would talk to him that evening, and I could come the next morning to learn the results.

I did not fail to keep the appointment, and found that he had been successful and was going to introduce me. We went together at once to see the commissioner. Either to amuse himself or to embarrass me, he asked me several questions, among others if I could understand and write English. "One as well as the other," I replied immediately. Then he said, "Sit down"—we were in front of his desk—"and copy this letter." I went at my task believing it to be a joke, because Captain Pouchot must have told him that I could neither speak or write English. I was careful to copy the letter that he gave me literally, doing my best to imitate the original. When I had finished, I gave him the copy. He found one mistake when he examined it. I was so positive that the error was not mine that I had the assurance to say so. This made him check the original, and the mistake was really there.

The commissioner began to smile at my audacity and determined manner, and surprised me agreeably when he said he was putting me in charge of the details of looking after the prisoners' affairs, and of paying for their rations. These were paid in money each week.

The matter of salary remained to be settled. I
asked for a piastre[5] a day and three shilling
for my board. But when the remark was made
that the other secretary got only a piastre for
everything, I agreed to that wage, for the very
good reason that I should have risked losing
the job if I had been too insistent in my
demand. I requested three days' leave, since I
would have to fetch my belongings. I consequently asked for my passport.

This request caused me to be questioned
about the place I came from, and how I succeeded on coming. I did not hesitate to tell
about my adventure, saying that it was the reason I wanted a passport. The commissioner
laughed at my frankness, and wrote me a three
days' permit with his own hand. I went to
thank my patron at once, and told him about the
interview. Then, going to my inn, I arranged
for my room and board at the rate I had paid
before-that is, three shillings a day payable
monthly.

I departed with my passport, stopping for
an hour in Jamaica, where I took my horse again
and went on my way. I encountered the same two
sheriffs who had chased me. They seemed to be
watching for my return. Since I no longer had
the same cause for fear, I let them approach.
They spoke to me; but as I could not understand
them, I really supposed that they were threatening me with prison, and saying I should not
get away this time. I took out my passport as
my safeguard to show them. One of them put out
his hand to take it, but I did not wish to
entrust him with it. My refusal made this man
strike me with his whip, I used a trick which
had already been successful on another occasion
and now occurred to me in this situation.

In Canada, I had learned to smoke. This
habit is common among all the people there.[6]   I

---

[5]Worth three francs in French money (JCB).
[6]Concerning the Canadians and smoking Kalm
reports, "Every farmer plants a quantity of

kept a pipe in a case made of very good hard-
wood and shaped like a pistol. I drew this out
and pointed it at the two sheriffs, as though
it were a genuine firearm. They halted immediately, while I spurred my horse and came to the
home of my host in a short time. He was surprised that I had been gone for three days, and
still more so when he saw the two sheriffs coming to his house. He did not know that they
were pursuing me. When they entered, they
spoke to him. For the first time, one of them
explained to me in poor French what they
wanted. Then I showed my passport which was in
order. But the affair of the pistol, which
they thought a breach of the law, remained. So
seriously did they stress this matter that I
let out a shout of laughter, snatched from my
pocket the object on which they accused me of
crime, and exclaimed, "There's the weapon you
are making much noise over. I really used it
to scare you, for I didn't know whether I had
encountered sheriffs or robbers trying to steal
my horse. I had no reason to think you were
sheriffs, since you two mistreated me. As one
of you speaks French, why didn't you speak to
me then? I should have understood him, and
could have answered. I do know that sheriffs
have no right to insult or mistreat anyone.
They have only the right to speak in the name
of the law, and to call for help in case of
resistance."

My argument was forceful, and the two
sheriffs were considered foolish after it was
talked over. They were cross about it but
withdrew quietly.

———————————————

tobacco near his house in proportion to the
size of his family. It is necessary that one
should plant tobacco, because it is universally
smoked by the common people. Boys of ten or
twelve years of age, as well as the old people,
run about with a pipe in their mouth. Persons
of the better class do not refuse either to
smoke a pipe now and then" (Kalm 1937:510).

I had to leave next morning to return to
New York. I asked for the same horse, but my
host was unwilling to lend him. I urged him,
and promised to pay him room and board for a
full month, though I had lodged there only nine
days. Finally, he consented, provided I would
promise to send the horse back next day. That
did not seem difficult.

I left an hour later-that is, about eleven
o'clock in the morning. I did not stop until I
reached the Long Island ferry. I planned to
leave the horse at the inn, but met a Frenchman
there who offered to take care of returning the
horse to his owner. I entrusted the horse to
him; how mistakenly will be shown hereafter.
Then I embarked, and arrived in New York at
four o'clock in the afternoon, going immediately to get settled in my hotel. The next
morning, I went to the commissioner's and
started at my job, to the great surprise of my
fellow secretary. I was to take care of paying
the prisoners, work he had formerly done.

Some days later, the host I had left came
to see me, and asked for his horse. Surprised
by this demand, I told him that I had asked a
Frenchman to return it and that he had promised
to do so. My astonishment obliged him to put
me at ease, by saying, "It is all right. My
horse is at home. The man you had take it is a
rascal, who abused your trust. I met him on
the road to Philadelphia with my horse, when I
was taking flour there. I went up to him and
asked where he got the horse he was leading.
When he gave me a poor explanation, I stopped
him and the horse, and took them to the first
justice of the peace I could find. There I
told my reasons. The man was immediately questioned. He replied that he had bought the
horse for ten guineas[7] from a man he did not
know. But as he could tell neither where he

---

[7]A guinea is worth 21 shillings and weighs
"deux gros douze grains." It has the same rank
as the French louis d'or (JCB).

had bought the horse nor the seller's name, the judge sentenced him to restore the horse with no compensation except three days' feed. I did not object to this, and paid him at once."

The man nevertheless scolded me for having trusted an unknown man too much, and said I might have had to pay for his horse. I knew I was wrong and said nothing. But to keep the man from being dissatisfied, I gave him a guinea for my room and board (as I had promised) and a piastre to repay him for the cost of the three days' feed for his horse. He was much pleased, thanked me, and left.

During the time I stayed in New York, I was witness to the barbarous way they punish negroes. This depends more or less on the whim of the slave's owner.

The Frenchman at whose inn I was living had among other servants a young negro, twelve years old, who was lazy and very greedy. The master had threatened to punish him several times. One day, he caught him in the act, eating food from dishes ready to be served. He gave him a box on the ear, and threatened to punish him later in the day. Though several of us interceded for him, it was unavailing. The little wretch, realizing his master's intention and fearing his severity, ran away from the house, hardly knowing where to find refuge. When the master became aware of his flight, he had him searched for everywhere. He was found and brought back to the house of his master, who locked him up for an hour. During this time, the master got a rod about two feet long and some ropes. Then he took him to a mound. Four of us followed him, more in the hopes of having the punishment mitigated than to be a witness. We saw him lay the victim out on the ground. The master tied the boy's hands together, passed the rod under his knees and elbows, tied both with ropes, ands fastened his head to the rod. He was stripped, and looked like a ball in this position. The poor wretch then received more than fifty lashes. In vain we begged for mercy for the victim, whose body was covered with blood. The master was piti-

less, and rolled him from the top to the bottom
of the mound with heavy blows from the whip.
Finally, he stopped beating him. The negro was
released and taken back to the house, where he
was washed and rubbed with oil and sugar.

I have been told that punishment is even
more severe in San Domingo. Humanity ought to
cry out against these punishments which belong
to barbarism rather than to civilized man.[8]

In December, the agreement between France
and England for the exchange of prisoners
reached New York. It had been made on February
6th, 1760. Several days afterward, the order
was given to get two transport vessels ready to
take back to France, the French prisoners in
and around New York. The first of January was
the date fixed for their departure.

During this interval, I was able to finish
the triple accounts of the expenses of all the

---

[8]The trade in negroes is carried on in
Senegal, in the Congo, in Kaffirland, in
Guinea, in Nubia, and in Nigeria, which are
parts of Africa. These Africans, always at war
among themselves, have never sent out any
formidable conquerors. There lack of
civilization has left them with neither
intellect or judgment. They are coarse,
shameless, and lazy, especially in Nigeria, and
greedy for our alcoholic liquors. Yet they are
kind to strangers. From Nigeria to the Cape of
Good Hope, the blacks traffic in women, while
fathers sell their children and children their
fathers. Some of the tribes eat their
prisoners. They maltreat captives worse than
do Europeans to whom they sell them. Some Arab
tribes called Moors live among them. They are
located near the rubber forests, and keep
Europeans away. The negroes have priests
called Marabouts. The Portuguese have tried to
civilize the Congo by introducing Christianity
there, but the Congo is still the same. From
Nigeria to Senegal there is trade in rubber,
gold, elephants' tusks, etc. (JCB).

French prisoners from the time they were captured. According to these accounts, the expense amounted to eighty thousand one hundred and thirty-nine francs and fifteen sous for six hundred twenty-five prisoners, counting each one from the day he was taken prisoner up to January first, the day of departure. While I was figuring up the accounts and making a correct copy, the commissioner, who was employing me, made me a handsome offer to stay on. But as I was more eager to return to France, and, besides, did not understand English, I declined his offer with thanks.

On December 31st, the day before sailing, all the prisoners were put on board ship. Instead of six hundred and twenty-five carried on the rolls, only five hundred and four embarked. Therefore, one hundred and twenty-one men remained in this country voluntarily, all regular soldiers, for the Canadian prisoners were free to return home.[9]

---

[9]It is estimated that 107 marine officers and 1052 soldiers returned to France. It is likely that these men were those who had been in the colony for a short time and were serving in central Canada. The men at the western posts probably settled in the Mississippi River valley or worked in the fur trade.

XVIII

Year 1761: On the first of January, the
officers and I went on board the *James*, a six-
hundred-ton vessel commanded by Captain Cooper.
Three hundred men were being carried in this
ship, not counting the commissioned officers.
The other ship called the *Boscawen*, was a small
two-hundred-and-fifty-ton vessel commanded by
Captain Nobster. This small vessel carried the
rest of the prisoners.

The west wind came up two hours after we
had gone on board. We raised anchor and set
sail, starting on our way to France. All went
well enough for the first five days.

On the sixth, we ran into a fierce storm
which separated the two boats. We had to lie
to for five days. We lost sight of the
Boscawan, after we had seen her tossed about by
the tempest for a long time, and so believed
she must be lost. We were still more certain
of this when we did not see that ship again
during the rest of the trip. We faced a similar danger, for the ship *James* was an old boat
that shipped a great deal of water. We had to
man the pumps day and night during the entire
voyage. The sea became calm three days later,
and for four days we went on sailing easily
enough. Then, a contrary wind forced us to
tack about for several days.

On the 20th, we had another storm which
made us ship still more water, and made the
vessel leak in two places, so that we feared it
would break apart. Then, we and our belongs
would undoubtedly have been lost. Fortunately,
no other leak appeared in the boat, and that
was the last storm we encountered; for if we
had had another storm, we should have lost all
hope of seeing France again. This was the
crew's opinion-they did not conceal their fear.
Despite our anxiety, we continued our voyage,
not daring to crowd our sail and put too much

strain on the boat. We had to inspect it constantly, and continually pump out the water,
which, even with this precaution, rose in the
hold to the depth of a foot and a half.
Finally, after forty days of sailing, we were
brought, for some unknown reason, to the harbor
of Portsmouth instead of a French port.

On February 15th, we dropped anchor in
this haven, where, at the time of our arrival,
there were eight hundred vessels anchored. We
were kept there for ten days, which were tedi-
ous for us.

We left on the 26th, and reached Harve on
the 28th. We anchored a league from the city.
We could not approach nearer because of the
current of the River Seine, which is felt in
the sea near its mouth for almost that distance.

On the first of March, some barks came to
take us to shore. We were much surprised to
see the prisoners whom we had thought lost with
the ship *Boscawen*. We had not seen it since
the 6th of January. They had arrived two weeks
before us, and had had the same fear for us.
With this thought in mind, they had a mass said
for us a week after they arrived. We thanked
them and, wishing to show our gratitude,
invited them to a feast which took place on the
fourth. The feast lasted a whole day, and next
day the greater number set out on their own
road homeward.

It may be noted that all the free companies of the Marine coming from Canada were discharged at Harve by government order. Each
individual was given a full discharge with
thirty francs to take him home. As some soldiers had several years' pay due them, the government ordered eight months' pay on account
given them. It was different with the troops
of the line. They were ordered to rejoin their
regiments by short marches.

Personally, I had three years' pay coming,

at the rate of eighteen francs a month.' For
the three years, this made a total of six hundred and forty-eight francs. Like the others,
I received eight months' pay on account, which
made a hundred and forty-four francs. I
received thirty francs passage-money. These
two amounts together made one hundred and
seventy-four francs. I brought with me from
New York seven hundred francs in French money,
which I had saved without knowing if I could
ever redeem it

   This was the extent of my fortune when I
arrived in France. I converted this money into
gold at Harve before leaving, so that I should
have less weight to carry on the way.

   I left Harve the 14th, and arrived in
Paris the 22nd. My first thought was to go and
look for my family, whom I had lost sight of
for ten years. I rejoined my father and mother
with great pleasure, and decided to stay with
them, sharing the little money I had left.

   I sought to convert my four thousand paper
francs into money. This could only be done at
the bourse, where I went with that intention,
and where I was obliged to agree to a rate of
twenty per cent. Thus four thousand francs
brought me eight hundred francs in cash. This
pleased me very much, but not without reminding
me that I had made a poor bargain in New York
when I gave a five hundred franc note of this
same paper money for ten guineas, or nearly two
hundred and forty francs in French money. It
would have been more profitable if I had kept
them until my arrival in Paris, but it was too

   'This suggests that J.C.B. served as a
corporal in the artillery, although he never
mentions attaining that rank. His service as
storekeeper may have required that he be
considered a non-commissioned officer. It is
interesting that he is claiming pay that does
not take into account deductions for rations or
equipment. This may be due to the lack of
supply late in the war.

late now and my thoughts on this subject were
useless.

As I had moments of leisure while staying
with my father and mother, I began to review
and rearrange the manuscript of my travels.
Since then, I have revised and had them read by
several people, who advised me to make them
public and have them printed. I could not make
up my mind, when I considered how much time had
elapsed since these travels, and how few people, perhaps, would be interested in knowing
the facts about a country which no longer
belongs to the French. I feel, however, that
the facts in these travels may interest people
intending to travel in Canada, and even those
who merely want to know more about the country.

It seems certain that since my voyage
there have been many changes in Canada; as much
in population, which naturally has increased,
as in places of settlement, the new routes of
communication, the clearing of ground, the
felling of trees, and finally a soil which is
more productive since the English took possession. I have been told by people coming from
the country that the English in Canada have
changed the names of many villages and those of
the rivers, lakes, and savage tribes; among
others the names of the Iroquois tribes.

Yet some things a modern traveler will
always recognize and cannot be changed; such as
locations of lakes, rivers, towns and villages
which existed at the time the country was lost,
as well as the distances between them, and the
customs of the Canadian habitants, and of the
savages even when they are civilized. It must
be admitted that the process of civilization
will be long and difficult; as much from the
extent of the country as from the remoteness of
the most savage people, and from their sense of
independence; for most of these tribes now
enjoy unhampered freedom. The five Iroquois
nations are an example. Missionaries have been
working among them since the early days of the
French settlement in the colony, but there are
very few converts among them, though they do
revere some saints. Still another obstacle is

the fact that the English of Canada, as well as
the Anglo-Americans, are unjust and shifty in
their dealings with the savages-a very poor
policy.

I may also note that the English in Canada
and the Anglo-Americans of the present-day
United States can use a method to civilize the
savage peoples different from the religious
efforts made by the French. They can be
fairer, bring them near the inhabited parts by
distributing land allotments for them to cultivate in full-ownership, and give them everything necessary for this. They can trade with
them for the surplus of their harvest and for
their furs. By the establishment of police in
every village and settlement, civilization will
gradually and firmly be established.

It is true that, since the establishment
of the United States, the population has been
increased a great deal by the immigration of
families from various European countries.
These have been given land to clear and cultivate in many places. This is especially true
along the banks of the Ohio, where towns and
villages have sprung up, as well as in two new
states, Kentucky and Tennessee. Kentucky, formerly a district dependent on Virginia, borders
the east bank of the Ohio. Tennessee, once
part of North Carolina, extends from the
Appalachian or Allegheny Mountains to the bank
of the Ohio, and stretches as far as Georgia,
under the name of the Government South of the
Ohio.[2] These two regions were absolutely unin-
habited in my time, but seem to be well populated at present. Though the people are of
various nationalities, self-interest and the
need for social life draw them together, causing them to make family ties, and, in this way,
to become ever more sociable.

The same thing will happen west of the
Ohio in the section called Scioto, where many

---

[2]He appears to confuse Tennessee with the
Southwest Territory (PHC).

similar allotments and free grants of land have
been made. it is also possible to settle some
savages there, but on the contrary, they try to
drive them out by buying the land the savages
own and occupy. This seems unwise.

Another unquestionable fact is that the
English of Canada have as yet done nothing to
gain the goodwill of the Canadians, who are
keeping their French sympathies and making it
only too apparent. Doubtless for this reason
the English dislike them, and perhaps this is
why they have changed the names of various
places and of several savage tribes. But the
Canadians, ever confirmed friends of the French
and therefore fixed in their habits, still call
them by their old French names and even refuse
to speak the English language. The English
attitude toward this makes it seem that they
are somewhat indifferent about keeping Canada.

XIX

These travels have made mention, in passing, of the way savages engage in war, their alliances, preparations for war, dances, and war feasts; of their precautions taken when they have decided on war; of their way of fighting, surprising their enemies and scalping them; of the treatment of prisoners, either adopting, enslaving or burning them; and, also, how they travel in winter, and of their taste for liquor.

It now remains for me to tell about their physique, character and swiftness in running; about their way of living, clothing, marriage, women, and childbirth; about their children, homes, and councils; about their weapons, games, funerals, tombs, and mourning; about the way they designate the months and moons; about the four mother tongues of those tribes; and, lastly, about their gods.

Their Physique

Generally speaking, the savage peoples do not keep any hair on their bodies. It is not easy to say why they keep it only on the back of their head. There it is cut short, leaving one or two long strands, dyed black, which they braid and let hang to their shoulders. There is none on the rest of their body, for they are careful to pluck it. Some even pull out the eyelashes and eyebrows, as well as any down on the body. It stops growing in a few days for no known reason. Some old men, however, have some hair on the chin. They claim that lack of hair results from the abundance of blood, which is purer because of their simple diet, and which produces fewer excess substances.

There is little doubt that their simple diet makes the savages swift runners. Still more certain is the fact that the savages con-

sider it a great mark of beauty to have no
hair, except on the head. Perhaps this is more
a matter of custom than of beauty. If any hair
grows, they take care to pull it our immediately. They are usually tawny. Thus, far from
portraying them as hairy, savages should with
more truth be shown naked except for a loincloth.

Many savage tribes are accustomed to tat-
too the whole body. Others are satisfied with
painting the face and body in different colors,
first rubbing themselves with bear grease, and
then daubing on black, red, blue, and green.
This is an ordinary decoration for them.
Often, when they are at war, they use it, they
say, to frighten or intimidate their enemies.
One might more easily believe it is to hide
their own fear, for they are probably not
immune to it. They also paint prisoners black
when they intend to kill them, as well as
painting themselves black when they return from
war after losing some of their men.

Their method of tattooing is to trace the
figure or design they wish to make on the skin
stretched taut. When a man wants to have his
whole body tattooed, he is stretched on a
board, and the tattooer begins to mark out as
much as can be done in one sitting. Next, he
pricks him with little needles, arranged in a
row and fastened firmly between two thin pieces
of wood. This instrument has six to twelve
needles which are carefully arranged to stick
out at most two to three lignes. He dips the
points of these needles in the color desired,
which is prepared either from alder charcoal or
gunpowder; from red earth or vermilion; or
blue, green, and the like; all bright colors.
They are mixed with water or oil, after first
having been well ground up.

When the needles are wet with the dye, the
marks or patterns are pricked back and forth,
taking care to did the needles frequently in
the color used for the tattooing. As the blood
must flow from the part thus cut by the
tattooer's stroke, a swelling follows, forming
a scab which falls off after a few days. Then,

the wound is healed, and the tattooing or pat-
tern stands out clearly. The healing takes a
shorter or longer time, depending on the amount
of tattooing done. It is very curious to see a
man tattooed in this way, especially when the
entire body is tattooed in colors. I have seen
an officer who had been tattooed in this manner. He spoke several savage languages. They
thought well of him, and often used him as an
interpreter.

Most of the Indians split the ends of
their ears from top to bottom, without cutting
the edge which hold them together. They bend a
long flat lead strip through and around the
length of the slit. The weight of the lead
naturally stretches the flesh. When it is
healed, they remove the lead and substitute
brass wire twisted like a corkscrew, and bent
into a half circle as large as the opening.
This amounts sometimes to five or six inches.
When the man walks, this flaps and looks like a
pump going up and down. Often, the weight of
this insert pulls the upper part of the ear
loose, and when this happens, they let the
piece dangle, which looks horrible. But
whether left hanging or not, the savages tie
the two ears together behind the head, when
they go to war or go hunting, so they will not
be hindered in running. It is only when they
dress up that they let their ears hang. Then
they put feathers and pieces of fur dyed various colors into the wire. This makes a plume
on each side of the head.

The women are unlike the men, in the first
place, by being very proud of their hair. They
keep it long, full, and shiny; taking care to
rub it frequently with bear grease which thick-
ens it, and covering it with powder made of
rotten wood. They make it as large as one's
fist, then wrap it with eel or snake skin.
This pigtail is flattened on the back, and
rounds a little higher up. As their hair very
often grows long, they turn it up halfway down,
making the pigtail thicker, and as large at the
bottom as at the top. In the second place,
they as a rule, do not make slits in their

ears, but often pierce several holes in them
for jewelry, whenever they can get it from the
men. This is easy enough for them when they
inspire love, for they always take advantage of
it.

Their Character

The character of these peoples is a mixture of simplicity and trickery, nobility and
meanness, vanity and politeness, good nature
and treachery, valor and cowardice, and humanity and barbarity.

A savage is ferocious. In his fury he
breaks the laws of nature. When he feels he
has been injured, he is capable of going three
hundred leagues or more to surprise his enemy,
and satisfy his revenge with blood.

As to vices, the most common are the mistreatment of women and indulgence in liquor,
which has been mentioned before.

Usually the savages are properly obedient
to the old men, chiefs, and war leaders.

Perhaps no nation in the world scorns
women more than these savages usually do. The
bitterest insult that can be offered a savage
is to call him a woman. They are, however,
usually very jealous of their wives.

Their Swiftness in Running

They are generally fleet of foot. The
Illinois and Missouris are reputed to have the
best legs. It is claimed that they outrun
bears, buffaloes, and even deer. I cannot ver-
ify this statement; but I have seen a footrace
on the Ohio shore near Fort Duquesne, where
several runners raced with some Illinois and
Missouris, and these latter were easy winners.
It is said—it may be a mere story—that an
Illinois once was seen driving a deer before
him and pursuing him all day long. He guided
it with a switch as far as his village, where
it was captured and killed.

Their Way of Living

They live in separate households. The woman always does the cooking, the main thing being to cook maize or grain and fresh or smoked meat from the hunt. Sometimes, the maize is cooked alone after it has been well pounded, and makes a pudding which is called sagamite. The women also soak this grain in lye, by boiling it with ashes in a kettle of water. Then, they take it out, wash it thoroughly, and dry it in the sun. By this time, it is whiter and more tender, having lost the yellow skin when it was soaked. Again, the women make the earthen jars or bowls, and the wooden spoons they call "micouens." The latter are shaped like a soup spoon, but even larger, and with a short curved handle that can be hooked onto things. The spoon bowl and handle are made of one piece of wood; the handle is attached to the edge of the middle of the oval bowl.

As the savages are abstemious enough to know the value of fasting, they eat only one meal a day, of the sort just described. They, however, make up for this very frequently, either when the corn is young and tender with milky ears which they eat just as it is; when the wild fruits are ripe; or when they go hunting. Very often, in this last case, they take a piece of the slain animal, and stick it on a spit driven in the ground before a fire built with poles above it to smoke or cure the game. When the piece of meat is cooked on one side, they turn it around and eat the roasted side while the other is still cooking. This is called "appola."

Their Clothing

The older custom, which still exists among the remoter savage tribes, is to wear skins of the wild beasts they have killed. These skins are thoroughly scraped and rubbed with the animals brains or fat, together with rotten wood made into powder. Then the skins become soft

and pliable, and they use it for clothing and
bedding.

The tribes in contact with Europeans,
selling furs to them, gladly wear shirts,
woolen clocks, loin cloths and leggings. They
get all these in exchange for their furs, or
are given them when they are hired to fight.
On their feet they wear a covering made of
deerskin, scraped, rubbed, and smoked, which by
this process, becomes as supple as tanned
sheepskin. The women prepare the skin, and
make the shoes for the men and for themselves.
These shoes, which the savages call
"mockassins," are gathered at the toes and are
sewn above and behind with a raised flap on
either side. This is turned down over the cord
below the ankles which ties on the shoes.
Often these folded edges, as well as the front
and back of the shoes, are decorated with ribbon or dyed porcupine quills of various colors,
with red predominating. Sometimes, they add
some glass beads and tiny copper bells, which
are either round or long and trumpet-shaped.

The loincloth is made of deerskin or of
cloth obtained from Europeans. It is a quarter
or a third of cloth that the men wind between
their legs. This piece of cloth is held in
place around the hips with a cord. The two
ends of the loincloth are folded over in front
and in back, with the end on front longer than
the one in back.

The women dress like the men, save for
their head dress, which was explained before
when I told of the men's physique, except that
they wear a skirt of deerskin or cloth instead
of a loincloth. This goes around the body, and
is folded double over a belt or cord around the
hips. This skirt, called a machicote, reaches
only to the knees, and often has ribbons for
decoration or ornament around the bottom, as
well as porcupine quills and little bells. The
women also wear bracelets and collars of porce-
lain beads around their necks and arms. To add
a finishing touch, they paint their faces with
red vermilion which they buy from the
Europeans.

Their Marriages

Polygamy is established in several savage tribes. Among the Algonquins, it is common enough to marry all the sisters in a family; a custom based on the notion that sisters get along better with each other than with strangers, and in this case they are all on the same footing. Among the true Algonquins, there are two classes of wives. The second class are the servants of the others. Some of the savages have wives at every place they stay when they are hunting. Among the Iroquois in general, there is even confusion because of polyandry.

In some tribes, the men are very scrupulous in regard to the degree of relationship and its bearing on marriage. One must not marry a relative; but if a wife dies first, her husband must marry her sister, or if she has no sister, must marry a woman selected by the family of the deceased. A wife, for her part, is obliged to do the same thing as far as her husband's brothers or relatives are concerned, if she has had no children and is still young enough to have any. A husband who refuses to marry the sister or relatives of his widow lays himself open to all sorts of insults from the woman he has rejected, and must suffer in silence. If there is no one left, a widow is allowed to seek elsewhere, but presents must be given to her, as witness of her good conduct during her first marriage.

Among all the savage nations, there are certain families recognized who can marry only among themselves. There are agreements to stay together as long as they are happy, and to separate when they tire of one another. There are others, in which a husband who leaves his wife without good cause must expect retaliation from the wife's family, and a woman who leaves her husband without being compelled by his mistreatment will have a bad time of it.

Among the Miamis, the husband has a right to cut off the nose of a wife who runs away. Among the Iroquois, Hurons, and others, they may separate by mutual consent and, sometimes,

two friends will exchange wives to increase
their happiness.

Mutual jealousy most commonly disturbs the
peace of the family. The Iroquois are exces-
sively jealous. When a woman discovers that
her husband loves another, her rival had better
beware; especially as the faithless husband
dare not defend her in any way, without dis-
honor. It is the same among the Loups,
Shawnees, and others.

Marriages are usually arranged by the parents. Those made through libertinism must be
excepted. The parties concerned do not appear;
yet, final arrangements are made only with
their consent.

Among some tribes, the girls are urged not
to marry, for they are permitted as many trial
marriages as they wish.

The prospective bridegroom always gives
the wedding presents; such as the halter,[1] the
kettle, and a fire log. The halter means that
the wife must carry the burdens; the kettle,
that she will do the cooking; and the log, that
she will provide not only the wood, but everything else necessary for the household.
Whatever her duties may be, the new husband
also has his duties; such as hunting, fishing,
and war. He must also build a cabin, if he has
none, and make a mat for his wife to sleep on.
He must keep the cabin where they are living
repaired.

The wife, for her part, gives her husband
only a bag of fragrant red leaves, which she
gathers in the woods and dries out thoroughly.
This is for her husband to smoke. Usually
these dried red leaves are mixed with tobacco,
and make it very sweet. It needs to be sweet,
for the savages almost always have pipes in

---

[1]This halter must not be confused with the
wampum belts mentioned in the course of these
travels. It is the sort of halter mentioned in
connection with the *traine* (JCB).

their mouths. They call this mixture "petun" or "sumack."

In some other villages, the bridegroom need only go and sit down in the cabin beside the girl he wants for his wife. If she permits it, she keeps her seat. Then, he throws her bits of wood he has been busy cutting, that are a little thicker and longer than matches. If the woman accepts them, the marriage is complete. The man goes out at once to the woods, and his wife follows.

The women cultivate the ground and do the sowing and harvesting. The crops consist of maize, beans, pumpkins, and watermelons. Sometimes, the men help with the harvest, which ends in a festival lasting far into the night.

The men glory in their idleness, save for hunting, fishing, and war. Yet, the women often help them in these three tasks; first by carrying the game, which is a very common practice, and by mending their shoes, which is always necessary.

The woman bear children, usually unattended and without pain but always away from their cabins, in little shelters built for this purpose forty or fifty days previous in the woods, or sometimes in their fields. If it happens-it rarely does-that a woman has a delayed labor, the young people are called, and they come and make loud yells near her, when she least expects it. This give her a sudden shock which often causes delivery.

Their Children

These mothers nurse their own children, sometimes two at a time. They care for them, and carry them on their backs with a small board twenty-five or thirty inches long, bent at the upper end like the traines I have described. On it, a pad of cotton is prepared, and the baby lies there on his back with the pad folded over him. Then, this is fastened with straps, and carried with the child's head upright under the plank's curved end. If it is a boy, the mother takes care to fix a small piece of bark like a gutter to catch the urine and carry it off, which keeps him from wetting himself. Otherwise, the child is changed whenever necessary.

When it leaves the cradle, the child is not interfered with in any way. He is given complete liberty to roll about on his feet and hands, in the woods, in the snow, and even in the water, when he is strong enough. He learns to swim like a fish. All this helps a great deal in making these children strong, supple, and agile. Ordinarily, when they are three or four years old, their mothers leave them to themselves; not through harshness and indifference, but because they believe nature must be let alone and unhampered.

Bows and arrows are put in the hands of children at an early age, and they become expert in their use in a very short time. They are made to fight each other, and, sometimes, one would be killed, if care were not taken to separate them. The losers are so ashamed, that they do not rest until they have revenge. For this reason, they seem born with a desire for glory.

The only education children receive is by hearing their mother and father tell the brave deeds of their ancestors and their tribe. They become enthusiastic over these stories, and grow up and imitate what they have been taught to admire. Kindness is used in correcting them, never threats. If a girl behaves badly, and her mother is sensitive about honor, the mother weeps. If the daughter asks the reason, she then says only, "You are dishonoring me." This answer is often sufficient for a girl who has any feeling of shame, though this situation is rare.

The giving of a name ends the period of early infancy. The ceremony is carried out with a feast attended only by persons of the same sex as the child that is to be named. He is held on his mother's knee, and given the name of a dead warrior in his family.

Children are usually thought of as belonging more to the mother than to the

father. Since they are brought up with this
notion, they respect their father only as the
master of their cabin.

Their Homes and Councils

A village has no regular plan. It is a
group of cabins of various shapes and sizes.
Some are as long as a shed. They are all built
and covered with tree bark, with the exception
of a strip in the roof about two feet long, to
let out the smoke from a fire of the same size.
On each side of a cabin, there are beds made of
bark spread on sticks and raised seven or eight
inches above the ground. The exterior of these
cabins is sometimes covered with a mixture of
earth and brush to keep out the wind. The
doors are likewise of bark hung from the top
like blinds, or fastened on one side with
wooden withes, making a swinging door.
In general, savages fortify better than
they house themselves. Villages may be seen
stockaded like redoubts, making provision for
water and stones. The piles and the stones
used to build them have battlements able to
withstand a siege. But they must live near
their enemies and fear being surprised, if they
entrench themselves in this manner.
Each village has its own chief. His only
powers are to assemble the young men when war
is to be made, and to reply to an invitation
for an alliance. In each village, there is
also a sorcerer or wizard. As savages are
superstitious, they place great trust in their
wizards and look upon them as oracles.
There is only one wizard to a village,
usually an old man. He gets ready for his
duties by steam baths. They make a little
cabin of tree branches stuck in a circle on the
ground, bending the upper ends over and across
one another. It looks like a huge beehive.
They cover it with wild animal skins or wool
blankets, and then put a red hot stone inside.
The wizard goes inside with some water, which
he pours on a stone. This causes a dense
steam, which makes him perspire. When he has

perspired a great deal and feels weak, he comes
out and jumps into the water to wash himself.
Then, he comes back to deliver his prophesy,
which tells he warriors who have consulted him,
if they will be successful or be defeated in
war; if they will lose any men; if they will
take prisoners and scalps; and finally tells
each one how far he must travel.

They undertake no war and make no treaty
without first holding council among themselves.
This council decides whether war is to be
undertaken, and, in that case, the war chiefs
urge the young men to take up the hatchet
against the common enemy, whom they try to surprise.

Regarding these councils, Dr. Franklin has
observed that, as the people do not know how to
write, the women learn by heart the discussion
carried on.   He says the women as well as the
children attended these councils.   I am not
completely in accord with that except for the
Iroquois, whom Dr. Franklin had perhaps seen in
council because they are the nearest to
Virginia and Pennsylvania.   I have never seen a
village council of those tribes, but I have
seen them in council with the French.   Then the
women did not attend.   The tribes in the north,
west, and south are not accustomed to introduce
women into their councils in any way.   If that
were true, it would be inconsistent with the
scorn they have for women.   I, nevertheless,
quote from his statement.

"The savages," he says, "are accustomed to
keep much order and decency in their assem-
blies, since they have frequent occasion for
holding public councils.   The old men sit in
the front row, the warriors in the second row,
and the women and children in the last.   The
women's task is to note with care what is done
in the councils, engraving it on their memory,
and teaching it to their children to be handed
down as tradition, for these people have no
writing.   They are the council registers, and
keep the remembrances of treaties made a hundred years ago.   When we compare what they say

with our written records, we always find them exact.

Their Weapons

Originally, the only weapons that the savage had, were the bow and arrow, with a sort of spear having a point of bone fashioned in various ways, and a two-foot club made of very hard wood with a rounded head which had one cutting edge. When they were at war, attacking the enemy and the enemy's stronghold, they protected themselves with reed mats, or mats made of thin pliable strips of green wood, wrapping these around their bodies to shield them from the blows they received. The savages of the far north still use these weapons, and have shields made of buffalo skin or bear skin stretched around a hoop. These protect them from arrows.

Since the greater part of these tribes have become acquainted and familiar with Europeans, they have grown accustomed to firearms. They use them in preference to their own arrows.

The Dutch brought the first supply of firearms, small hatchets, and knives. The first to get them were the Iroquois. The French followed the Dutch and the English in doing this. These weapons became a necessity, which perhaps maybe regretted. For many of these tribes now use only firearms, as well as the small hatchets called tomahawks, and knives for which they have many uses, especially for scalping. As a result the arrow is used only by children, to develop their skill. Although the savages use firearms, they are very particular when they select these weapons. They try several to find a good one, especially if they are buying them.

When savages go to war, they are armed with guns, tomahawks, and knives. They usually have three knives; one hung around the neck, one in the belt, and one fastened in the garter on the outside of the leg. Canadians arm them-

selves in the same way, as a precaution of
safeguard.

Their Games[2]

The dish game is simple. It is played
with peas in a wooden dish or bowl. Several
peas are made to jump in the air without letting them fall on the ground. If they do fall,
the player loses the game, and his opponent
takes whatever stake there is.

The game of knucklebones is for two persons only. Each one has six or eight
knucklebones, with six unequal sides. The two
larger sides of these are painted; one black,
and the other yellowish white. The dish in
which they are placed is spun around, and then
struck on the table to make the pieces jump.
If all the knucklebones that fall show the same
color, the player wins five points. The game
is forty. The winner keeps on playing and when
he loses, gives way to another player.

The game of straws is played with little
pieces of grass, the size of wheat straw, two
or three inches long. A bundle of two hundred
and one straws is made. They are shuffled well
and then dropped. Next they separated with a
pointed piece of bone into piles of ten. Each
player takes his at random and the one getting
a pile with eleven wins a point. The game is
for sixty or eighty points. Any number of persons, up to twenty, may play it.

The game of lacrosse is played with a bat
and a ball. Two posts are set up for the
bounds, the distance between them depending on
the number of players. For example, if there
are sixty or eighty players, they will be
nearly half a league apart. The players are
divided into two teams, and each has a post.
The ball is hit to the opposite side, which
bats it back without letting it fall to the
ground or touching it with the hand. If it

---

[2]This heading is inserted (PHC).

does fall to the ground, or is touched by a hand, that side will lose the game. Savages are so skillful in batting the ball, that the games sometimes last several consecutive days.

Their Funerals, Tombs, and Mourning

Savages are very reverent toward the dead. Mothers have been known to draw milk from their breasts and scatter it over the tombs of their children. This is, however, not usual. If a village where there are dead bodies takes fire, they are the first to be taken to safety. Savages strip themselves of their most precious possessions to adorn the dead. The dead man is dressed in his best clothes, his face is painted various colors, and beside him are placed his weapons, powder, lead, a hatchet, a knife, and all his belongings. He is thus laid in his grave, with food, a kettle, tobacco, and his pipe; everything, as they say, to make the great voyage and hunt in the land of spirits. When everything is in place, the body is so covered that the earth does not touch it. It is wrapped in skins that are adorned with feathers. The earth is raised like a pyramid, and sometimes a post is placed over it, which set forth his brave deeds—if it is a warrior's grave—and the esteem men had for him. Some tribes have the custom of carrying food every morning to the dead. Dogs and other beasts take advantage of this. But the savages are persuaded that the souls of the departed come and take this food.

After the interment, presents are given to the family of deceased. This is called "attending the dead." These presents are given in the name of the village, and sometimes in the name of the tribe when he was a noted chief or a great warrior. But before that, the family of the deceased gives a feast in his name, then has games, jousts, and races. The family of the dead man does not participate.

For mourning, they have all their hair cut off, blacken their faces, and wrap their bodies in blankets, without speaking or making any

visits, and thus depriving themselves of all
pleasure for about six moons.   Men never weep
because, according to savages, tears are unwor-
thy of men.   But women weep for their husbands
and children for a long time, three times a
day; morning, noon, and sunset.   The chiefs
mourn for only six moons.

Their Way of Naming the Months and Moons.

Savages divide the year into twelve moons.
When there are thirteen moons, the last one is
called the lost moon.   Each moon gets a name
from the weather.   For example, March, considered the first month of the year, begins with
the first new moon after the spring equinox,
and is called the month of worms, because grubs
then come out from their winter retreat.   April
is the sower's moon;   May the flower moon; June
the warm moon; July the deer moon; August the
sturgeon moon; September the wheat moon;
October the travelers' moon; November the beaver moon; December the hunting moon; January
the cold moon; and February the snow moon.
In this way, the names these tribes give
the moons or months are taken from nature
itself.   This is not surprising, as physical
phenomena must always have been the first thing
to impress these peoples from the moment when
they first noticed natural occurrences.   If the
savages' division of the year is neither very
exact nor in accord with astronomical observa-
tions, one must admit, however, that the names
given by them to each part of their division
are much wiser and more reasonable than the
names adopted by Europeans.

The Four Mother Tongues of the Indian Tribes

The Sioux, Algonquin, Huron, and Iroquois
are the four mother tongues of the savage
tribes.   The Sioux language is spoken northwest
of the Mississippi.   Algonquin and Huron in
central Canada still are shared by most of the
northern tribes.   Whoever knows these two languages can make himself understood among the

many tribes.   Iroquois, which is spoken in
southern Canada, is also understood by many
northern tribes.

Their Divinities

Each savage tribe, even each village, has
its own tutelary god, called Okis and Manitou.
They are the symbols which represent the guard-
ian spirit of each one.   Most savages wear
their symbols around their necks, and, if they
travel on the water, put them in the fore part
of their canoes as a safeguard against acci-
dents.

Okis and Manitous are only the forerunners
of the Great Spirit, which is God.   To make
them favorable, savages give them offerings,
throwing into a lake or river tobacco and,
sometimes, birds they have strangled.

Algonquins and Hurons call the chief
Spirit the Great Hare.   Other tribes call him
Michabou, and still others, Attahourans and
Matromec.   The Hurons call him Areskoui.   The
Iroquois named him Agreskoui, while others give
him the name of Nossou and Sakeschat.   All
these names mean Sovereign Master, the Great
Spirit of God, God of War,-in short, a benefi-
cent God, more perfect than all others.

Appendix

Indian Tribe Mentioned in these Travels[1]

Abenaquis, they are composed of several scattered tribes which are: the Canibas, the Souriquois, the Micmals, the Montagnes, the Malecites, and the Amalecites. All these tribes except the Canibas were the first savages to ally themselves with the French. They are native to Acadia which the greater part have left to come to the vicinity of Quebec. These men are numerous, brave, and warlike.

Ackancas, inhabitants on the Mississippi, are fine-looking men.

Agniers, one of the five Iroquois tribes south of Canada, always strongly attached to the English. They persecuted the missionaries most, but have produced Christians and martyrs, nevertheless.

Ajoues, live on the Mississippi.

Alibamons, of Louisiana, friendly to the English.

Amalecites, tribe of Abenaquis.

Amikoues, nation of the beaver, north of Lake Huron.

Andostes, tribe of Hurons whom they have left.

Asnipoels, near Hudson Bay in Lower Canada.

Aticamegues, live in the north of Canada

Baygoulas, of Louisiana, few in number.

Berciamites, of Tadoussac on the St. Lawrence River.

---

[1]Actually, this list includes some tribes not mentioned in the Travels. The translation preserves the original's forms for the names of the tribes, and the original's alphabetic arrangement and cross-reference (PHC).

Biloxis, of Louisiana.

Bissiriniens, in the north of Canada.

Canibas, tribe of Abenaquis.

Cenis, on the Mississippi.

Chactas, of Louisiana.

Chats, tribe of Eries in the north.

Chaouanons, of the Ohio.

Cherakis, on the Mississippi.   The English call them Chiroques.

Chetimachas, of Louisiana.

Chicachas, of Louisiana.

Colapisas, of Louisiana.

Cristinaux, near Lake Superior.

Eries, to the north of Lake Erie, destroyed by Iroquois.

Eskimaux, on the coast of Labrador.

Folavoines, fine-looking men near Michigan.

Goyongoins, tribe of Iroquois south of Lake Erie.

Hurons, they live in several parts of Canada. This nation, proud and independent, is industrious and warlike.   It has always been friendly to the French.   In most councils they speak first, having superior ability and a noble language.   They have sustained cruel wars with the Iroquois, who could not conquer them.

Illinois, a numerous nation in the north of Louisiana, great runners and bold thieves, but enemies of their neighbors because of the corruption of their morals.

Iroquets, nation in the heart of Canada.

Iroquois, this name is French; the proper name is Agononciosi, which means "builders of cabins."   This nation lives in the south of Canada from the heights of Montreal to the Ohio.   It is proud, haughty, and jealous.   They were the first to be armed with guns.

Kappas, of Louisiana.

Kicapoux, near Lake Michigan.

Loups, or Mahuigaus, on the banks of the Ohio.

Mahuigaus, see Loups.

Malomines, see Folavoines.

Mascoutins, or Fire Nation, neighbors of the Malomines and Kicapoux.

Miamis, or Ouyatanons, near Michigan.

Micmaks, tribe of Abenaquis.

Mingos, of South Carolina.
Mississagues, in the north of Canada.
Missouris, of Louisiana.
Mistassingues, in the north of Canada.
Monsonis, in the north of Canada.
Montagnes, tribe of Abenaquis south of the St. Lawrence River.
Natches, of Louisiana, grow good tobacco.
Natchigamis, the same.
Natchitoches, the same.
Nippissingues, tribe of Algonquins in the north of Canada.
Noquets, of Hudson Bay.
Octatas, near the Missouri.
Offongoulas, of Louisiana, allies of the Yazous and Chicachas.
Omas, in Michigan.
Oneyoutes, tribe of Iroquois near the Ohio.
Onontagues, tribe of Iroquois near the Ohio.
Osages, of Louisiana.
Otchagras, or Puants, on Lake Michigan.
Outagamis, or Renards, in the north of Canada.
Outaouas, very numerous on Lake Huron.
Ouyatanons, tribe of Miamis.
Oumamikoukas, at Tadoussac below Quebec.
Panis, of the north, the first to use the calumet.
Papinachois, near Tadoussac.
Pinitouis, of the Illinois.
Plat Cote de Cheins, in the north of Canada.
Pouteouatamis, near Michigan.
Puants, see Otchagras.
Poux, they are the same as the Pouteouatamis.
Renards, see Outagamis.
Sakis, near Michigan.
Sauteurs, between Lake Huron and Lake Superior.
Savanois, in the far north.
Sioux, numerous warriors northwest of the Mississippi.
Souriquois, tribe of Abenaquis.
Tamarouas, tribe of Illinois.
Tetes Plates, near Michigan.
Tetes de Boule, Algonquins.
Themiscamings, the same.
Tionontathes, tribe of Hurons near Detroit.
Tioux, near the Natches.

Tonikas, of Louisiana.
Topingas, tribe of Akancas.
Torimas, the same.
Tsonontouins, tribe of Iroquois.
Yazous, allies of the Chicachas and Offongoulas.

BIBLIOGRAPHY

Bonin, Jolicoeur Charles. *Travels in New France by J.C.B.* S.K. Stevens, Donald H. Kent, and Emma Edith Woods, Editors. Harrisburg: Pennsylvania Historical Commission, 1941.

Bougainville, Louis Antoine de. *Adventure in the Wilderness*. The American Journals of Louis Antonie de Bougainville 1756-1760. Edward P. Hamilton, editor and translator. Norman: University of Oklahoma Press, 1964.

Costain, Thomas B. *The White and the Gold*. Garden City: Doubleday and Co. Inc. 1954.

De Lery, Gaspard-Joseph Chaussegros. *Journal of Chaussegros de Lery*. Harrisburg: Pennsylvania Historical Commission, 1940

Eccles, W.J. *The Canadian Frontier 1534-1760*. Albuquerque: University of New Mexico Press, 1974.

Gallup, Andrew and Donald Shaffer. *La Marine, The French Colonial Soldier in Canada 1745-1761*. Bowie, MD: Heritage Books, Inc. 1992.

Hamilton, Charles. *Braddock's Defeat*. Norman: University of Oklahoma Press, 1959.

Hamilton, Edward P. *The French and Indian Wars*. Garden City: Doubleday and Company, Inc., 1962.

Harrington, J. C. *New Lights on Washington's Fort Necessity*. Richmond: The Eastern National Park and Monument Association, 1957.

Kalm, Peter. *Peter Kalm's Travels in North America*. New York: Wilson-Erickson, Inc. 1937.

Kent, Donald H. *The French Invasion of Western Pennsylvania.* Harrisburg: Pennsylvania Historical Commission, 1954.

Knox, John. *The Seige of Quebec.* Mississauga, Ontario: Pendragon House, 1980.

Morse, Eric W. *Fur Trade Routes of Canada, Then and Now.* Toronto: University of Toronto Press, 1979.

O'Meara, Walter. *Guns at the Forks.* Englewood Cliffs, N.J.: Prentice-Hall Inc., 1965.

Stone, Lyle M. *Fort Michilimackinac 1715-1781.* East Lansing: Michigan State University 1974.

INDEX